HEALTH REPORTS:
DISEASES AND DISORDERS.

OBESITY

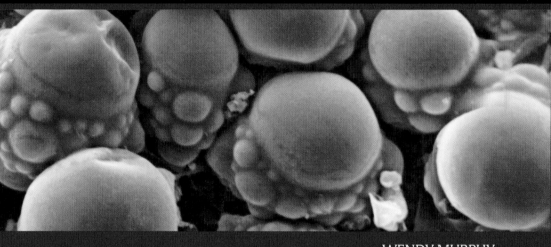

WENDY MURPHY

TWENTY-FIRST CENTURY BOOKS
MINNEAPOLIS

To Jessica, who inspired me with her courage, resolution, and triumph

Cover image: This micrograph shows fat cells filled with lipid droplets. These fat cells store energy as an insulating layer of fat.

USA TODAY®, its logo, and associated graphics are federally registered trademarks. All rights are reserved. All USA TODAY text, graphics and photographs are used pursuant to a license and may not be reproduced, distributed or otherwise used without the express written consent of Gannett Co., Inc.

USA TODAY Snapshots®, graphics, and excerpts from USA TODAY articles on pages 6, 8, 13, 16–17, 18, 20–21, 29, 32–33, 45, 49, 54–55, 60–61, 62, 65, 68–69, 72, 76–77, 81, 82–83, 92–93, 100 © copyright 2012 by USA TODAY.

Twenty-First Century Books
A division of Lerner Publishing Group, Inc.
241 First Avenue North
Minneapolis, MN 55401 U.S.A.

Website address: www.lernerbooks.com

Library of Congress Cataloging-in-Publication Data

Murphy, Wendy B.
    Obesity / by Wendy Murphy.
        p. cm. — (USA Today health reports: Diseases and disorders)
    Includes bibliographical references and index.
    ISBN 978–0–7613–6086–5 (lib. bdg. : alk. paper)
    1. Obesity—Popular works. I. Title.
    RC628.M85 2012
    616.3'98—dc22   2011001251

Manufactured in the United States of America
1 – MG – 7/15/11

CONTENTS

USA TODAY.
HEALTH REPORTS:
DISEASES AND DISORDERS

CHAPTER ONE

EATING TO LIVE

NICK'S STORY

I've been big all my life," says fifteen-year-old Nick Roemer. "By the time I entered sixth grade, I already weighed 250 pounds (113 kilograms) and had to shop in the oversized department. I'm taller now, but I'm heading for 300 pounds (136 kg) soon, and it seems like I am constantly hungry.

"After school I spend a lot of free time by myself. I don't much like sports, I suppose because I'm not very good at any of them. So I'll stop on the way home at one of the fast-food places and get a soda and a snack to tide me over. From then until dinnertime, I do homework and play video games in my room. To tell the truth, life at home is kind of disorganized and depressing.

"My mom, who is pretty fat herself, usually comes home from work too tired to prepare real meals. So she'll order Chinese food or a large pizza for the two of us, and we eat without talking much, just watching TV. Neither one of us ever mentions my weight, but going to school has become a nightmare. I hate to raise my hand in class and— maybe I am imagining it—my teachers seem to pick on me. Most of my classmates avoid me. I would give anything to get out of my situation, but I feel stuck."

Nick's story has become more and more common. By some estimates, two-thirds of adults and nearly one in three children in the United States are overweight or obese. In 2001 U.S. surgeon general David Satcher called excessive weight a public health crisis and introduced his *Call to Action to Prevent and Decrease Overweight and Obesity*. His successor, Regina Benjamin, announced a plan to

Over the past fifty years, more and more people in the United States and other industrialized countries have become overweight.

expand this program in 2010. In the surgeon general's *Vision for a Healthy and Fit Nation 2010*, Benjamin stated that "the prevalence of obesity, obesity-related diseases, and premature death remained too high."

A half century ago, a very small percentage of young people were overweight. Most households did not regularly snack on foods like potato chips, french fries, and nachos. And no one had video games or home computers. Young people spent more time outdoors and were more physically active. The working lives of adults were likely to be physically demanding too, since fewer people worked in office jobs. The lifestyles of young people and adults have changed a great deal in the recent past.

Americans have decreased their physical activities while consuming more calories. Experts estimate that women consume 22 percent more calories and men consume 7 percent more than they did about forty years ago.

This book takes a close look at this recent development, explains the reasons it's happening, and examines the health costs of being overweight. You will also see what people can do to maintain a healthier body through balanced eating habits and better lifestyle choices.

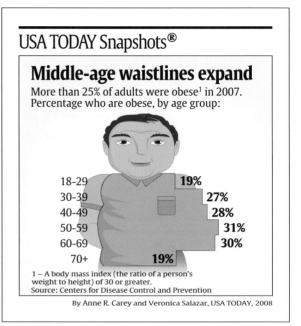

USA TODAY Snapshots®

Middle-age waistlines expand

More than 25% of adults were obese[1] in 2007. Percentage who are obese, by age group:

Age group	Percentage
18-29	19%
30-39	27%
40-49	28%
50-59	31%
60-69	30%
70+	19%

1 – A body mass index (the ratio of a person's weight to height) of 30 or greater.
Source: Centers for Disease Control and Prevention

By Anne R. Carey and Veronica Salazar, USA TODAY, 2008

MEASURING WEIGHT

Until fairly recently, doctors paid little attention to their patients' weight or body type. Being "portly" or "stout" was a sign of wealth in the early twentieth century. Then doctors began to regard physical mass and body fat as important markers of health.

Weight measurement alone does not distinguish between pounds from body fat and those from lean body mass or muscle. Being overweight means having an excess of total body weight based on population averages for people of your same height and body type. Athletes and very muscular people may be overweight, but that does not mean they are obese. Obesity is an excess of body fat regardless of weight. Overweight and obese people are at risk for many serious medical conditions. For this reason, health-care experts have developed tools for measuring healthy weight and body mass.

The most widely used measurement of adult weight is body mass index (BMI), which measures your weight in relation to your height. A formula yields a number that provides more accurate measures of body fat. Belgian scientist Adolphe Quételet came up with the BMI method. Its calculations are based on the metric system of measurement (kilograms of weight and meters of height). The formula for calculating BMI is

$$BMI = \frac{\text{weight in kilograms}}{(\text{height in meters}) \times (\text{height in meters})}$$

To figure out BMI with pounds and inches, the result is multiplied by 703:

$$BMI = \frac{\text{weight in pounds}}{(\text{height in inches}) \times (\text{height in inches})} \times 703$$

For example, to calculate the BMI for a person who weighs 220 pounds and is 5 feet 7 inches (67 inches) tall, you would multiply 67 by 67 to get 4,489 inches and set up the following equation:

$$BMI = \frac{220}{4,489} \times 703$$

You divide 220 pounds by 4,489, which gives you 0.049. Finally, you multiply 0.049 by 703 for a BMI of 34.45.

Health experts say that, for adults, a BMI of 18.5 to 24.9 represents ideal weight. Research shows that people who have BMIs between 19 and 22 tend to live the longest. Adults with a BMI of 25 to 29.9 are described as overweight. And those with a BMI between 30 and 39.9 are termed obese.

A BMI of 40 or more usually means having more than 100 pounds (45 kg) of excess weight. Weight experts label people with BMIs in this range as morbidly obese. Their weight may be life-threatening because many health problems occur with this excess.

About one-quarter of all Americans are either obese or morbidly obese. In 2009 the U.S. Centers for Disease Control and Prevention (CDC) set out to determine the prevalence of self-reported obesity in each state. Only Colorado and the District of Columbia reported that less than 20 percent of their citizens were obese. In thirty-three states, 25 percent of the population was obese or morbidly obese. In Alabama, Arkansas, Kentucky, Louisiana, Missouri, Oklahoma, Tennessee, and West Virginia, the number was 30 percent or more. Mississippi weighed in with the highest proportion at 34 percent.

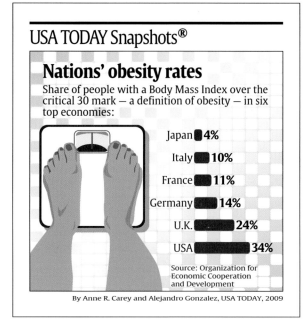

Millions of children and young adults are also at risk. Research shows that four out of ten children who are of above-average weight at four years of age will be obese as adults, unless something is done to change their habits. And the risk increases in adolescence. Eight out of ten teenagers whose BMIs exceed healthy limits are on the track to obesity in their adult years.

OTHER METHODS OF MEASUREMENT

Researchers found that BMI did not accurately measure body mass in children and adolescents. So the CDC developed the Percentile BMI system. This growth chart matches young people's weight and height with standards relating to age and gender. Children and adolescents who are close to the 50th percentile in weight are average. Those found to be at or above the 85th percentile for their group are considered at risk for becoming overweight. Young people at or above the 95th percentile are at severe risk for becoming overweight. A 2007–2008 survey by the CDC found that an estimated 17 percent of U.S. children and adolescents were obese. From 1976 to 2008, obesity increased from 5 to 18 percent in adolescents (ages twelve to nineteen).

Other, more accurate methods for measuring body fat include hydrodensitometry and dual X-ray absorptiometry (DXA). Hydrodensitometry uses a tank of water to weigh someone. Because the densities of bone and muscle are higher than water and fat is less dense than water, doctors can compare the weight of the person out of the water with the submersed weight. They use a standard formula to come up with relative fat-to-lean composition. In DXA, an X-ray machine scans the entire body and shows exactly where the fat is distributed.

Doctors also use skinfold testing. This is a kind of pinch test using a device known as a skin caliper.

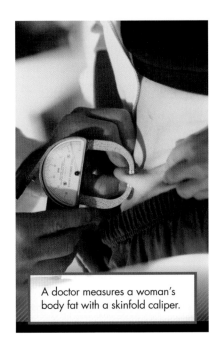

A doctor measures a woman's body fat with a skinfold caliper.

Skinfold testing measures the thickness of fat beneath the skin at certain points on the body and compares results with healthy norms.

HUNGER VERSUS APPETITE

Hunger is a physical drive directly connected to the body's need for energy. Appetite, on the other hand, is a desire for food. Hunger and appetite are not always in sync, however. Someone might genuinely need food to recharge his or her body. But, because of illness or depression or anxiety, that person may have no appetite. It's also possible for someone to be satiated, with all hunger needs fully met, but still have an appetite for certain foods. The latter is an emotional rather than a physical reaction. It may be triggered by a need for comfort or security or by boredom.

Nutritionists explain that many people overeat because they are no longer in touch with their natural appetite controls. Hunger is purely biological. Yet a number of triggers can stimulate appetite, including smelling, cooking, or seeing food. Even memories can make you crave a certain food. Sweet tastes and fat textures, both of which have higher-than-average energy potential, are especially tempting. Sometimes nutritionists refer to it as the pizza effect. Most people have a strong attraction to the combination of fat and sugar, as in peanut butter and jelly in a sandwich.

The medical community recognizes that other factors contribute to being overweight. But one cause remains clear. If you consume more calories than your body needs for growth, bodily repair, health, and energy, the excess turns into fat.

SATIETY SIGNALS

When your body is running low on energy, your gut sends out warnings in the form of hunger pains, or "pangs." Those pangs travel from your digestive system to your brain through the central nervous system. Your brain then sends out a signal that tells you to look for more food.

When your body has had enough food, you begin to feel full. Chemicals trigger that feeling of fullness—called satiation. These chemicals are released mostly in the gastrointestinal tract (the stomach and intestines) and to a lesser extent in the bloodstream. When these chemicals reach the brain, the hypothalamus (a cherry-sized region at the base of the brain) sends out a satiety signal. This signal tells you to stop eating.

Satiety signals and the sensations they cause are inner controls that the body uses to regulate appetite. It takes some time—an estimated twenty minutes—for the message to get to the

People often eat when they are not hungry. They may eat for social reasons. Other non-physical triggers may lead them to eat as well.

hypothalamus. People who eat quickly often consume extra food without realizing that they are no longer hungry. People who eat more slowly and with better dining habits (keeping regular meal times and not eating mindlessly in front of the TV, for example) are less likely to overeat.

ENERGY BALANCE

Babies respond almost instantly to their appetite controls. They take in just the amount of food they need to equal the amount of energy they expend. This is called energy balance. Later in life, people adopt eating behaviors and attitudes that have nothing to do with providing energy balance. And some people ultimately lose touch with their natural appetite controls.

Modern science has a very reliable tool to help keep track of just how well a person is managing energy balance. Both input (food) and output (activity) can be measured in calories. Calories are standard units that measure the potential heat energy stored in a substance, usually food.

To determine whether someone is maintaining a healthy balance, nutritionists compare the calories eaten as food with the calories expended to meet the physical and chemical demands of living over a period of time. In general, if you eat fewer calories than your body uses to do its work, you will slim down. But if you consistently eat more calories than you burn, your body stores the excess calories as fat, making your body heavier.

Calorie needs vary according to age, gender, and activity levels. On average, adults require about 2,000 to 2,200 calories daily to maintain a healthy energy balance. And if they get enough daily physical exercise to stay fit and strong, they burn up all the fuel they took in within a day or so. Exercise helps control appetite, uses up calories to maintain energy balance, and helps control excess fat. When it comes

to overall health, regular exercise also does the following:
- breaks down stored energy that otherwise is unused
- relieves stress and aids in relaxation
- counters anxiety and depression
- strengthens and tones muscles, the heart, and lungs
- enhances balance and flexibility
- improves the quality of sleep
- creates opportunities for social activities with friends and family
- improves self-image

Many Americans eat far more than the recommended number of calories and get little or no exercise. This creates an energy imbalance that leads to weight gain. Research show that 30 percent of Americans are sedentary, which means they are not physically active. They are not gaining any of the benefits of exercise, including avoiding weight gain.

Once a person gains weight, it is hard to lose it again—much harder than avoiding it in the first place. One pound (0.4 kg) of excess fat is equal to 3,500 stored calories. To lose that pound, a person must use up the extra 3,500 calories by decreasing food intake, increasing energy output, or a combination of the two.

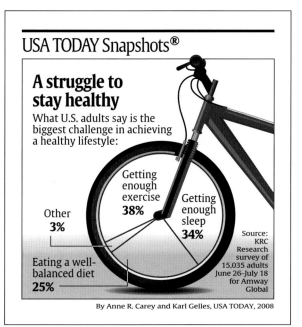

USA TODAY Snapshots®

A struggle to stay healthy

What U.S. adults say is the biggest challenge in achieving a healthy lifestyle:

Getting enough exercise **38%**

Getting enough sleep **34%**

Other **3%**

Eating a well-balanced diet **25%**

Source: KRC Research survey of 15,035 adults June 26-July 18 for Amway Global

By Anne R. Carey and Karl Gelles, USA TODAY, 2008

HOW MUCH EXERCISE DO YOU NEED?

The Centers for Disease Control and Prevention offers the following guidelines for staying fit:

Children and teens (ages six to seventeen) should get sixty minutes of physical activity every day. The following types of activity should each be included three days a week: vigorous-intensity aerobic activity (e.g., running); muscle strengthening (e.g., yoga, gymnastics); and bone strengthening (jumping rope).

Adults should get *at least*

- Two and a half hours of moderate-intensity aerobic activity every week plus muscle-strengthening activities on two or more days that work all major muscle groups (legs, hips, back, abdomen, chest, shoulders, and arms)

OR

- One and one-quarter hours of vigorous-intensity aerobic activity every week plus muscle-strengthening activities on two or more days a week

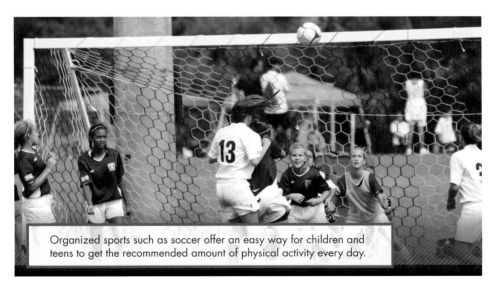

Organized sports such as soccer offer an easy way for children and teens to get the recommended amount of physical activity every day.

Yoga is a great way for teens and adults to strengthen and stretch muscles. Activities such as yoga are an important part of any health program.

OR
• A mix of moderate- and vigorous-intensity aerobic activity plus muscle-strengthening activities two or more days a week.

Meeting these goals can be difficult for some people due to busy schedules. The CDC suggests breaking activity into small chunks of time, about ten minutes in length (a ten-minute brisk walk three times a day, five days a week).

Aerobic activity (also called cardio) means you are breathing harder and your heart is beating faster. Intensity is how hard your body works during an aerobic activity. Moderate-intensity activities increase your heart rate and make you sweat. Moderate aerobic activity for non-athletes includes walking fast, swimming, riding a bike on level ground, and pushing a lawn mower. Vigorous activity means you're breathing hard and fast and cannot say more than a few words without pausing for breath. Vigorous-intensity activities include jogging or running, swimming laps, and playing basketball or soccer. Activities that strengthen muscles include lifting weights, working out with resistance bands, heavy gardening, and yoga.

www.usatoday.com

USA TODAY

News

SECTION A

February 9, 2010

From the Pages of USA TODAY

First lady says:
'Let's move' on child obesity

Her daughters were 6 and 9, and Michelle Obama was like any other working mom—struggling to juggle office hours, school pick-ups and mealtimes. By the end of the day, she was often too tired to make dinner, so she did what was easy: She ordered takeout or went to the drive-through.

She thought the girls were eating reasonably well—until her pediatrician in Chicago [Illinois] told her he didn't like the weight fluctuations he was seeing.

"I was shocked because my kids looked perfectly fine to me," Obama says. "But I had a wake-up call." Like many parents, however, "I didn't know what to do."

Today, the self-described "mom in chief" is launching Let's Move, a campaign to help other parents deal with a national health crisis she describes in epic terms. The goal: to eliminate childhood obesity in a generation.

"It's an ambitious goal, but we don't have time to wait. We've got to stop citing statistics and wringing our hands and feeling guilty, and get going on this issue."

She says she intends to "sound the alarm" about the epidemic: About 25 million kids are obese or overweight. Those extra pounds put kids at a greater risk of developing a host of debilitating and costly diseases, including type 2 diabetes, high blood pressure and high cholesterol.

Obama says she will use all the power of her White House pulpit to promote a multifaceted campaign that will include more healthful food in schools, more accurate food labeling, better grocery stores in communities that don't have them, public service announcements and efforts to get children to be more active.

Let's Move aims to do for healthy eating and exercise what the government's anti-smoking campaign did in the 1960s: change how people think about their health.

"The first lady having a huge microphone and a spotlight is really helpful," Health and Human Services Secretary Kathleen Sebelius says. "It's a big health crisis. We need to involve not only the kids but the families."

An ambitious plan

The campaign will begin the way many government efforts do: with the appointment of a federal task force that will give government agencies 90 days to figure out what they plan to do to help. Obama's office already has lined up commitments from mayors, business leaders, grocery store owners, school lunch suppliers, nonprofit groups, retailers and foundations.

Other elements of the plan, several of which will need approval in Congress because they require new funding or offer tax breaks, include:

- The American Academy of Pediatrics will encourage its 60,000 members to check the body mass index (BMI), a number that takes into account height and weight, of all children at every checkup, and to give every child a kid-friendly prescription with suggestions for healthy, active living at those visits, says Judith Palfrey, president of the academy. The group had been working on the idea, and the campaign "was the magic moment to roll it out with the blessing of the first lady," she says.
- $400 million in tax credits and other incentives to get grocery stores to move into "food desert communities" where people don't have access to major grocery stores and have to rely on corner markets, convenience stores and hybrid gas stations that may charge more and have fewer healthful choices. It will also get fresh foods into smaller stores.
- $25 million for schools to renovate their kitchens to replace deep fryers with equipment needed to store more produce and serve more nutritious food.
- $10 billion over 10 years for the Child Nutrition Reauthorization Act. Some of the money would be used to provide free and reduced-priced school meals for a million more children a year and to help schools serve more nutritious foods.

Agriculture Secretary Tom Vilsack says he's encouraging schools to "focus on community gardens and school gardens, which can provide additional supplies."

Healthful eating at school is important: About 31 million kids eat lunch at school every day, and 11 million eat breakfast. Overall, kids consume about 30% to 50% of their calories in school. Reports from the Institute of Medicine, which advises Congress on health and science, recommend booting junk foods out of schools and making dramatic changes in school meals.

Many companies are on board with improving school food, Obama says, by reducing the amount of salt, fat and sugar in school lunches and increasing the amount of whole grains and fresh produce. There are also changes to be made in the snacks provided to students.

"There is no reason why we can't have water, healthy juice drinks in vending machines, granola bars, trail mix, whole-grain sandwiches," she says.

Just as important as better food, Obama says, is physical activity. The government recommends that children get 60 minutes or more of physical activity daily.

Despite her lofty goals, Obama says, she wants to reassure fellow parents that they don't have to make huge changes or break the bank to have an influence on their kids' weight and health.

"We don't have to be 100% perfect," she says. If we get 20% of the way there, we will change the health status of our kids for a generation."

—*Mimi Hall and Nanci Hellmich*

HORMONES AND SET POINTS

An adult's body weight will generally stay the same, fluctuating only 10 to 20 percent over time. This weight range is known as the set point. Hormones and chemicals in the body help to naturally maintain the set point. When something happens that lowers body weight below the set point, such as a starvation diet or a serious illness, the body fights back to maintain the weight. Before modern times, the set point may have made humans better able to withstand drastic changes in their food supply. But most modern Americans don't have to worry about finding food over the long winter. For them, the set point has become a major obstacle to losing weight intentionally.

In the first days of a diet, pounds seem to come off quickly. But slowly the brain gets a signal that the body is in a state of famine (shortage of food). It slows down the body's chemical processes to make better use of the limited calories it has. This is the plateau that often occurs when someone is dieting. Further weight loss then occurs at a slower rate. This also causes dieters to easily gain weight back when the diet ends, even when they continue to eat carefully. The body is struggling to maintain a higher set point. Resetting the set point requires maintaining real changes to eating and exercise habits over several months.

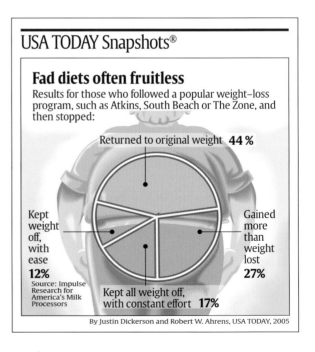

USA TODAY Snapshots®

Fad diets often fruitless

Results for those who followed a popular weight–loss program, such as Atkins, South Beach or The Zone, and then stopped:

Returned to original weight **44 %**

Kept weight off, with ease **12%**

Gained more than weight lost **27%**

Kept all weight off, with constant effort **17%**

Source: Impulse Research for America's Milk Processors

By Justin Dickerson and Robert W. Ahrens, USA TODAY, 2005

WHAT YOU'RE GETTING FROM YOUR FOOD

Carbohydrates, fats, and proteins supply 100 percent of the energy needed to do all the body's work. They all provide calories, but fat stores energy more efficiently. Therefore, it is more calorically dense.

Foods such as hot dogs and baked goods that are high in fat provide more calories per bite than do lean meats, fruits, and vegetables. An ounce (28 grams) of carbohydrates or proteins contains 112 calories (4 calories/g). An ounce of fat contains 252 calories (9 calories/g), more than double the calorie density of carbohydrates and proteins. Some foods are high in fiber, which provides roughage. Fiber works as a kind of internal scrub brush to cleanse the digestive system. Fiber also helps the body feel full for longer periods of time, even though it has no caloric value.

Foods with so-called empty calories, on the other hand, have little or no nutritional benefits and plenty of negatives. Candy, doughnuts, potato chips, and soft drinks are familiar examples of these unhealthy foods. Food additives are the salts, flavorings, preservatives, stabilizers, colorings, and other substances that food companies add to enhance appearance, taste, and shelf life of their products. Very few additives have nutritional value. For a healthy body, it's important to choose the foods that provide essential nutrients without unnecessary calories and additives.

Making good food choices at school and at home can help teens avoid empty calories.

www.usatoday.com

USA TODAY

Life

SECTION D

March 1, 2010

From the Pages of USA TODAY

Dieters hit that brick wall

After 10 pounds [4.5 kg] or so, it's hard to lose weight, especially in middle age

L osing weight is hard to do.
Especially for those who are middle-aged or older. After losing 10 pounds [4.5 kg] or so, they hit a brick wall and their weight loss stalls.

Cindy Groover, 54, of Palm City, Fla., who cut calories and walked 3 miles [5 kilometers] a day to lose 15 pounds [7 kg], says: "When I was young, I could drop 10 pounds [4.5 kg] in two weeks by going on a low-carb diet. These days, it just doesn't happen fast."

Tom White, 66, of Waukegan, Ill., who shed 17 pounds [8 kg] by cutting back on his food intake and working out regularly, describes himself as "a slower loser."

And Jonieta Stone, 68, of Scottsdale, Ariz., lost 11 pounds [5 kg] and says losing weight is "taking much longer and is much harder" than ever.

National obesity experts aren't surprised by the experiences of these three dieters.

Research shows that people usually drop about 5% to 10% of their starting weight in the first three to six months on a program. For many people, that's a loss of 10 to 20 pounds [4.5 to 9 kg]. After

that, some people hit the wall and their weight plateaus.

Losing this much is the "sweet spot" for many people, but if they "want to go beyond that 10% loss, there is going to be some pain and suffering," says Tim Church, director of preventive medicine research at the Pennington Biomedical Research Center in Baton Rouge [Louisiana]. "You are going to have to limit your calorie intake without starving yourself."

One reason it's difficult to drop more and keep it off is there's a cascade of biological responses designed to return dieters to pre-diet levels. A hunger hormone called ghrelin increases, and a fullness hormone called leptin decreases, research shows. In essence, your body defends its own weight, Church says.

And other factors are at work that may make weight loss more difficult for some people than others, such as genes, loss of muscle mass, lower overall levels of physical activity, deeply entrenched poor eating habits and changes in sex hormones, says Anne McTiernan, director of the Prevention Center at the Fred Hutchinson Cancer

Research Center in Seattle [Washington]. She has conducted several weight-loss studies with middle-aged people.

She says there could be some genetic variability in people's ability to hold on to or lose weight: "There are so many genes controlling this."

Changing levels of hormones, including estrogen in women, also affect weight as people age. Scientists at Pennington found women had lower metabolism after menopause than before.

The postmenopausal women in one study burned an average of 100 to 150 fewer calories a day just resting and doing their everyday activities, and they were less physically active for a total drop of about 200 calories a day after menopause, says lead researcher Jennifer Lovejoy, who now works for a health coaching company, Free & Clear, in Seattle.

The lower metabolism appears to have to do with changing levels of estrogen and not changes in muscle mass, she says. And there is evidence that a lack of estrogen increases appetite and can cause specific cravings for certain foods, especially carbohydrates and fats. That means women need to be careful about consuming too many cookies, cakes, candy bars and chips, she says.

Lovejoy recommends that women in their early to mid-40s begin gradually increasing their physical activity and watching their dietary habits to help offset metabolic changes that can lead to weight gain with menopause.

Keeping track

McTiernan says a major obstacle for many people is their life-long unhealthy relationships with foods and beverages.

"If someone is eating a bag of Oreos every night, that's extremely hard to change," she says. "They need to replace that habit with something else that will make them feel good. That's a big challenge."

Dieters who have the easiest time slimming down are those who need to modify only one or two unhealthy habits, she says—for instance, people who need only to stop drinking high-calorie beverages such as juice, regular soda or alcoholic drinks.

It's important to track calories either with a daily diary or log. Research shows that dieters who do that lose twice as much as those who don't.

After you lose weight and become smaller, you need fewer calories to maintain your smaller body, Church says. And that means you have to pump up the physical activity to get that negative caloric balance.

He recommends both calorie-burning aerobic exercise such as walking, jogging, biking and swimming, and strength training, which helps preserve lean muscle. And there's a big weight-loss advantage to physical activity. McTiernan's studies show that dieters who exercise in addition to cutting calories lose about 3 to 5 pounds [1.4 to 2.3 kg] more in the three to six months they are on a program than those who don't.

—Nanci Hellmich

NUTRIENTS

Certain quantities of key nutrients are necessary to maintain energy. Lack of these nutrients can lead to diseases that stunt growth and development. Consuming the appropriate amounts of key nutrients should not be difficult for most Americans. The problem lies in what we choose to eat.

Generally, nutrients are divided into two classes: macronutrients and micronutrients. Macronutrients make up the bulk of a healthy diet. They include proteins, carbohydrates, and fats. They are the source of calories in the diet. The U.S. Department of Health and Human Services' dietary guidelines recommend a healthy diet of about 55 percent carbohydrates, 30 percent fats, and 15 percent proteins.

Proteins supply amino acids, the building blocks that build, repair, and maintain body tissue. Foods from animals—lean meats, poultry, fish, eggs, and dairy products—are dense with proteins. These so-called complete proteins contain all nine essential amino acids. Beans, nuts, tofu (a soybean product), peanut butter, and grains are some vegetable sources of protein. People who consume vegetables as their only source of protein, such as vegetarians, must be sure to consume a well-balanced variety. Almost every vegetable protein lacks at least one essential amino acid.

Carbohydrates are the body's main source of energy or calories. They are either complex (starches) or simple (sugars). The body converts both kinds of carbohydrates to glucose (a form of sugar) and sends it through the bloodstream to every cell in the body. Cereals, vegetables, fruits, and sweets (snacks, sugary drinks, candies, and desserts) are the main sources of carbohydrates.

The third macronutrient includes fats and oils, the densest energy sources in our foods. Fats, also known as lipids, are made up of fatty acids. Some of these are more healthful than others. Unsaturated fats are healthy fats. Monounsaturated fats are found in plant

All fats are not created equal. Monounsaturated fats, such as those found in olive oil and flaxseeds, and polyunsaturated fats, such as those in walnuts and certain types of fish, are better for your heart than saturated fats.

foods such as olives, peanuts, and avocados. Polyunsaturated fats are found in seed oils such as corn oil, as well as in walnuts, almonds, cod, pink salmon, tuna, and sardines. Monounsaturated and polyunsaturated fats from vegetable sources are easy to recognize because they are liquid at room temperature.

Saturated fats, such as animal fat and butter, are solid at room temperature. Trans-fatty acids—found in margarine and other shortenings—are the least healthy form of dietary fat. They should make up less than 10 percent of our total calorie intake.

While fats can be harmful to the body, they are an essential part of our diet. Fats carry certain vitamins and hormones into and out of our cells. They contribute to making us feel full, so they help control our appetite. Fats that gather around internal organs and under the skin provide insulation. They help protect the heart, kidneys, and other body parts from hard blows and extreme temperatures.

Fats are the raw materials for building cell membranes (the linings of cells) and maintaining nerve function. Fats are especially important during infancy and the early years of growth when the brain is developing and expanding its network of connections. Fat is also a lubricant, helping our joints work more smoothly and our skin stay smoother and softer.

Micronutrients are the vitamins and minerals found in food. We only need small quantities of micronutrients. But they are essential to maintain a healthy body. Vitamins help control the chemical processes that take place in the body. The human needs thirteen different vitamins, which are best absorbed if obtained from food rather than from manufactured supplements. More than sixty minerals exist in the body, but only about twenty-two are essential for healthy body function. Of these, the minerals calcium, phosphorus, sodium, chloride, potassium, and magnesium are the most important.

CHOLESTEROL AND OTHER FATS

The two major fats in the bloodstream are cholesterol and triglyceride. Fats are energy-rich substances that serve as a major source of fuel in regulating the body's many chemical processes. They are essential in building and maintaining key parts of your cells, including cell membranes. Fats also play a role in the production of several essential hormones. Fats of all kinds are manufactured in the body, primarily in the liver. They are also found in many of the foods we eat, including eggs, meats, butter, cream, full-fat milk and cheese, poultry, and some fish.

To travel through the body where they are needed, cholesterol and triglycerides attach themselves to certain proteins and become lipoproteins. When the amount of these lipoproteins circulating in the bloodstream exceeds what the body needs or can use, serious long-term health problems may result.

Doctors monitor two types of lipoproteins in their patients: low-density and high-density lipoproteins (LDLs and HDLs). LDLs are commonly referred to as "bad" cholesterol because they have a tendency to form waxy deposits (plaque) on the interior walls of arteries and other blood vessels. As the plaque accumulates, it eventually narrows the space within an artery. This slows or even blocks blood flow to some parts of the body, including the heart and the brain. This condition is known as atherosclerosis. HDLs are often called "good" cholesterol because they tend to gather bad cholesterol as they travel, eventually carrying it away altogether. The role of excess triglycerides is still not entirely clear. High levels of these fats often go hand in hand with excessive LDLs.

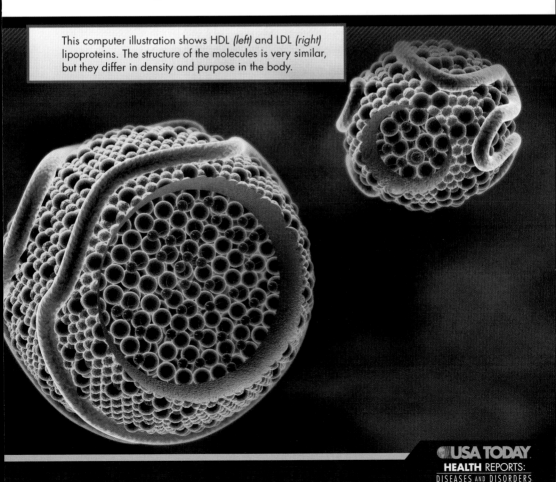

This computer illustration shows HDL *(left)* and LDL *(right)* lipoproteins. The structure of the molecules is very similar, but they differ in density and purpose in the body.

Doctors often use blood tests to determine the ratio of HDLs and LDLs, as well as the overall lipoprotein count. If the test indicates too little HDL or too much LDL, or if the total count including triglycerides is higher than desirable, there are several ways to lower the amounts. Strategies include dietary changes, such as adding more natural fiber, increasing physical activity, and lowering total dietary intake of fats. Medications such as statins, which block the manufacture of cholesterol in the liver, are also available if lifestyle changes are not enough to correct cholesterol levels.

METABOLISM

The average body burns 60 percent of its calories just staying alive. The body's resting or basal metabolic rate (BMR) is the sum of all the energy (calories) needed by the lungs to breathe; by the heart to beat; by the blood to circulate; and by the brain, kidneys, and other organs and systems to carry out their separate roles under normal, stress-free conditions. BMR includes the energy needed to maintain a consistent internal temperature of about 98.6°F (37°C) in a situation that is neither much warmer or colder that the body. It also includes the energy needed to grow new hair, nails, skin, and other cells as the worn-out ones die.

Another 10 percent of metabolic calories are spent in digesting food. Every time you swallow a spoonful of cereal or a bite of hamburger, your body has to break down, or digest, all the nutrients to a form that it can use. This is a fairly energy-intensive job. And the balance of calories—about 30 percent—fuel voluntary skeletal muscle activity, such as running, walking, chewing, brushing your teeth, and playing video games. Any calories that are not used in service to the BMR, to digestion, or to movement are changed into droplets of fat that are stored in the body's expandable fat cells as a form of condensed energy, where it stays until needed.

Metabolic rates vary from person to person. Some people seem to be able to eat high-fat foods and exercise minimally without gaining weight or developing other health disorders. Others eat less and still have trouble maintaining a healthy weight or keeping weight off after dieting. Factors influencing metabolic rate include hormonal and physical activity, gender, age, and certain envi-

This micrograph shows a fat cell with a large lipid (fat) droplet giving it volume. The small orange droplets surrounding it will combine to form one large lipid droplet.

ronmental factors such as climate. Inheritance may also play a part.

Professional athletes have a much higher metabolic rate than other people of the same age and gender. Tour de France cycling champion Lance Armstrong consumed an average of 6,500 calories daily to maintain strength. He ate up to 10,000 calories per day on peak days bicycling up mountains in France to fuel the increased demands on his body.

Metabolic rates vary with gender. In general, females have slower metabolisms than males. Rates also vary with age because of the amount of physical growth that may be going on. Allowing for small differences, a typical three-year-old needs 1,300 calories to maintain health and vigor. A child between the ages of seven and ten needs about 2,000 calories per day. The calorie consumption appropriate for girls and boys eleven to fourteen is 2,200 and 2,500 calories, respectively. For fifteen- to eighteen-year-olds, it is 2,200 and 3,000, assuming that these youngsters are physically active.

Metabolic rates slow as people mature and their physical growth ends. So by the age of twenty-five or thirty, people must begin to reduce the total number of calories they eat. Otherwise, they are likely to gain at least 10 pounds (4.5 kg) per decade even if they stay physically active. In later adult years, caloric requirements go down again. Active middle-aged women require about 2,000 calories and men about 2,200. The numbers are even lower for people who do not exercise. The age-related decline in BMR is associated with a loss of lean body mass (muscle).

Metabolism is even influenced by climate, because burning fat is one way the body stays warm. The reindeer herders of Siberia, Russia, for example, can eat 2.5 times more fat than their herding counterparts in warmer southern climates. The Siberians are able

This Siberian reindeer herder will have a high metabolic rate because of the harsh climate in which he lives. Metabolic rates are also influenced by genetics, activity level, gender, and age.

www.usatoday.com

USA TODAY

Life

SECTION D

October 13, 2010

From the Pages of USA TODAY

Lower metabolic rate raises risk of gaining it back

The calorie connection: At the start of Season 8 of NBC's *The Biggest Loser*, the contestants' resting metabolic rate—the calories the body burns at complete rest—was 2,679 calories a day. By the end of the season, their resting metabolic rate was 1,890 calories a day.

Although a large drop in calories is expected because the contestants are much smaller in size and require fewer calories to move around, this drop was 500 calories more than would have been predicted, says Darcy Johannsen, a researcher at the Pennington Biomedical Research Center in Baton Rouge.

"This is what we call the metabolic adaptation. It's the body's way of conserving energy," she says. "Their bodies fought to conserve energy in the face of the large energy deficit created through the combination of low calorie intake and huge calorie expenditure from the workouts."

This means the contestants are "at an increased risk for gaining the weight back if they do not continue to exercise and/or restrict calories," she says.

This large drop in calories they need to consume each day may explain in part why some former contestants have regained weight, she says.

—*Nanci Hellmich*

to maintain cholesterol levels that are 30 percent lower than the average herder far to the south because they burn so much fat staying warm in winter months.

For all people everywhere, a nutritious diet and regular exercise are essential to maintaining a healthy body weight. But every body is unique, with different requirements for staying in balance.

CHAPTER TWO

NATURE, NURTURE, AND BODY WEIGHT

JERRY'S STORY

Twelve-year-old Jerry Abrams weighs 150 pounds (68 kg). His parents are concerned. They consult Dr. Engelman, Jerry's pediatrician, for advice, hoping to be reassured that Jerry will grow out of his "baby fat" when he enters puberty. Dr. Engelman first measures Jerry's weight and notes that it is up 20 pounds (9 kg) from his previous visit, just six months earlier. He does some quick comparisons with the growth chart he keeps on his desk. He finds that Jerry's weight puts him well above the normal range for his age.

Dr. Engelman observes that Jerry's mother and father are also overweight. He asks a few questions about the family's eating and exercise habits and finds that they're average. He then asks about the parents' own adolescent experiences with weight gain. He learns that both parents have struggled with weight problems all their lives. The doctor explains that given his age, weight, and his parents' body types and history, Jerry's current odds are running 10 to 1 that he will become an overweight adult.

But if Jerry is willing to make healthier food choices and to swap some of his TV time for more physical activity during his fast-growing years, he can trim down to a lower weight without going on a restrictive diet. Dr. Engelman sets a goal for Jerry to lose 1 pound (0.45 kg) a month. Most boys Jerry's age normally gain about 10 pounds (4.5 kg) a year as they grow taller. By losing at this modest rate, Jerry can comfortably achieve a healthy weight within a year. But, says Dr. Engelman, Jerry must also commit to maintaining the new healthier practices after he trims down. Being overweight is clearly part of his genetic inheritance. He will have to deal with it for the rest of his life.

Being overweight tends to run in families. If a child's parents are heavy, the child's risk of becoming overweight is fifteen times greater than if both parents are slim. But how much of that risk is due to genetic inheritance (nature)? How much is due to environmental circumstances (what biologists call nurture)?

The food choices parents make for their children and the atmosphere that surrounds the dining experience in the home influence a child's physical development. Attitudes of the community about personal appearance and physical activity may also contribute. Families don't just share their genes. They also tend to share the same diet, economic circumstances, and lifestyle habits.

All of these factors contribute to the way we grow and put on weight. The more researchers study the question, the more complex the relationships between body type, food, genes, environment, and psychological factors seem to get. We need to go all the way back to the beginning of human history, about two million years ago, to understand eating habits and how they have changed.

Parents have significant influence on the weight of their children—both through genetics and environment.

www.usatoday.com

USA TODAY
Life
SECTION D

March 1, 2010

From the Pages of USA TODAY

A 'call to action' on teen obesity

Experts say parents must set example and nurture healthy habits early

Obesity is proving to be a heavy burden for the nation's kids and teens. Experts have known for years that hauling around extra pounds takes a huge toll on children's health. It puts them at increased risk for type 2 diabetes, high cholesterol, sleep apnea and other health problems.

A study in 2005 found that children today may lead shorter lives by two to five years than their parents because of obesity.

About a third of children and adolescents in the United States weigh too much. With so many overweight children, some experts worry that the majority of this generation will be overweight or obese as adults.

A study in the *Journal of the American Medical Association* found that heavy teens often gain a lot more weight in their 20s. Half of obese adolescent girls and a third of obese teen boys become morbidly obese (80 to 100 pounds [36 to 45 kg] overweight) by their early 30s, the research shows.

"This new study should be a call to action to parents to look in their pantry and clean out all the junk food," says Keith Ayoob, a registered dietitian who works with overweight children and their families at Albert Einstein College of Medicine in New York.

Families need to eat better, he says. "If kids aren't eating fruits and vegetables daily, they aren't eating a healthy diet. Period."

He says he never sees children who have better eating habits than their parents.

Parents may think they can get away with making unhealthy choices, but the kids are watching, says Bethany Thayer of the American Dietetic Association. "If parents are being good role models, that can have a huge impact on what a child does."

Getting healthier should be a family affair, says Elizabeth Ward, a registered dietitian in Reading, Mass. Parents shouldn't single out overweight children and tell them they are too heavy and need to change their ways, but the entire family should work at eating better and being more physically active, she says.

Ward, the mother of three girls and author of *The Complete Idiot's Guide to Feeding Your Baby and Toddler*, recommends that parents:

- Eat meals as a family as often as possible. Families that eat together tend to have healthier diets than those who don't, Ward says. And meals made at home tend to be higher in fiber, fruits, vegetables and lower-fat dairy products than restaurant meals.

- Encourage children to find healthful recipes. Have them search magazines, cookbooks and the Internet for recipes, she says. You want them to get involved so the changes stick, she says. "You won't get far with an overweight child or teenager if you don't engage them in the process."
- Don't keep soda in the house. Drinking soda decreases the consumption of low-fat and non-fat milk, which contain important nutrients children don't get enough of, including calcium, vitamin D and potassium, Ward says.
- Don't keep a smorgasbord of snacks at home. Just keep one or two so nobody feels deprived, she says. "I buy 100-calorie fudge bars. No child needs more than about 100 calories for a treat. Treats are extras, not foods to grow on."

"If you have a variety of chips, three kinds of ice cream and three types of cookies at home, it's going to be harder to resist your child's request for those foods. There are going to be way too many opportunities to overeat."

- Become more physically active as a family. Go walking, biking, hiking or skating, Ward says. Some overweight kids are self-conscious about being physically active on their own, but they may be more comfortable with their parents. "It shows the child you care about his fitness, but you also care about your fitness and you value physical activity."

—*Nanci Hellmich*

Eating together as a family tends to help family members eat in a healthier way. Meals at home also tend to be healthier than those in restaurants.

EVOLUTION OF THE HUMAN DIET

Early humans lived about two million years ago. They existed before people raised cows and other livestock for food, before farmers planted and harvested crops, and before people developed towns of any kind. Early hunters had few tools or other belongings and moved from place to place on foot. They were constantly searching for enough food to stay alive.

In some ways, early humans were remarkably similar to modern people. They had the same sturdy organs, such as the heart, lungs, kidneys, the liver, and the pancreas. They had the same basic skeleton of bones and joints, held together by the same sets of muscles. They had a nervous system that made them see, hear, taste, touch, and smell in much the same way modern people do. And they had a digestive system like that of modern humans, able to convert foods into the energy needed to keep them alive and moving.

Early humans differed from modern humans in their lifestyles and diets. Scholars of early history call these people hunter-gatherers. Depending on where in the woodlands and the grasslands (savannas) they lived, these people became experts at hunting game, spearing fish, and gathering wild plants. They spent almost every waking hour figuring out where to find the next meal. When their efforts failed, everyone went hungry. Then, when someone made a fresh kill or came upon a great source of fruit or edible plants, they ate until their stomachs could hold no more.

Over the years, early humans walked many thousands of miles to follow the migrations of birds and animals and the seasonal ripening of wild fruits and vegetables. With few exceptions, our ancestors had to be tough to survive with little comfort or security. Tribal members who could not manage this hard life tended to die young, often before they were old enough to have children. The hardier people could keep going from feast to famine. They passed along their

Hunter-gatherers, such as the ones portrayed in this Mexican painting, spent most of their time seeking food to eat.

natural strengths to their children and their children's children. And so it went, for thousands of years. The people best adapted to the environment survived. They shaped the physical and biological traits of the generations to come.

THE EARLY HUMAN DIET

Scientists who study early human bones and teeth think that the typical diet for millions of years was quite different from the modern Western diet. Hunter-gatherers ate a diet higher in protein. About one-third of their diet was meat and fish. The meats were low in fat because they came from animals that traveled over hundreds of miles and were very muscular and thin.

Early humans consumed their mothers' milk in infancy. They rarely, if ever, tasted milk or milk products later in life. Wild mammals were hard to capture and even harder to hold still long enough to milk.

Our ancestors ate few grain-based foods. Wild cereal grains were tiny, hard to collect, and barely digestible without being ground into flour and cooked. Early people didn't have the time or tools to prepare food in that way. The only sugar they ate came from wild fruits and the occasional honey left by wild bees.

Early peoples used vegetable oils as medicine rather than for food or cooking. The only salt early people ate was found naturally in wild meats and plants that took salt from the soil. People did, however, eat a wide variety of wild berries, nuts, roots, sprouts, and leaves. And they enjoyed wild birds' eggs when they could find them.

In good times and when the weather cooperated, the early human diet provided a fairly well-balanced mix of the three basic macronutrients. Proteins came mostly from wild meat, fish, eggs, and nuts. Carbohydrates came from the fruits, roots, and other plants. And the fats were found mostly in meat and fish but also in some wild plants.

The ancient hunter-gatherers ate a great deal of dietary fiber from foods such as fruits, leafy plants, and seeds. Fiber kept early humans' digestive tracts running smoothly. It also gave them a feeling of fullness even when they didn't have much food. Their diet provided three dozen or so vitamins and minerals. When some part of the food supply failed, the weaker people developed nutritional deficiencies. Some died of malnutrition.

Early humans led extremely active lives. They may have needed to eat an average of 3,000 or more calories each day to fuel their energy output. Not much changed for nearly two million years. But sometime before 10,000 B.C., new patterns emerged.

THE BEGINNING OF FARMING

Too much hunting thinned the herds of wild animals. For this reason, hunter-gatherers began to eat more wild plant foods. When people found fertile stands of wild cereal grasses and other plants growing along their travel routes, they protected the plants. Then they returned each growing season to take care of the best-producing plants. They weeded out the poor producers.

Over time, people noticed that the protected grasses grew bigger and tasted better. Instead of moving on at the end of their seasonal harvest, they stayed to cultivate the land and ensure a fixed supply of food. They were the first farmers.

These early farmers also learned to domesticate cows, goats, sheep, pigs, chickens, and other animals. And for the first time, cereal grains and dairy products became staples of the changing human diet. But even though food supplies had become more reliable, most people continued to experience physical hardship.

Early farming was as physically demanding as chasing after wild game and looking for wild foods. Farmers constantly struggled to maintain energy balance. Our ancestors had to get at least enough energy from the foods they ate to equal the amount of energy they used. They had no knowledge of calories, much less ways to count them. But they recognized hunger by the weakness they felt when they ran short of food.

About 10,000 b.c., groups of people living in the Middle East began to develop more advanced methods of farming. This was thanks, in part, to the invention of better stone tools. They began to reap larger harvests with less labor. But people continued to spend much of each day working hard to get food. As a result, they remained lean and trim.

Early humans often died young of infectious diseases and other conditions. But scientists say these people were less likely to develop diabetes, high blood pressure, heart disease, and cancers. These are all common diseases and conditions of modern life. They are traceable at least in part to modern diets.

THE FARMING REVOLUTION

The human diet truly began to change in the 1800s, during the Industrial Revolution in Europe and North America. Several events occurred in the nineteenth and twentieth centuries that changed the rules of food supply and demand.

Farming became more efficient, thanks to the invention of labor-saving farm equipment. Food became less expensive and more abundant. Scientists developed food preservation and refrigeration technology, as well as better transportation systems. Foods that previously spoiled within days of harvest could be shipped to places hundreds or thousands of miles away.

Over a two-hundred-year period (1800 to 2000), Americans went from eating fresh and locally raised food to eating food produced on vast industrial farms. Most modern meats, for instance, no longer come from lean animals that eat whatever they find in

This reaping machine was created by Patrick Bell in the 1820s. Farming equipment such as this reaper helped farmers increase productivity and thereby lower the cost of food.

the pasture where they roam free. Most come from grain-fed sedentary animals that farmers raise to be tender, plump, and juicy. The meat that comes from these animals is usually high in fat.

Food processing and refining was another big change in the Western diet. Before the development of these processes, people ate vegetables, fruits, and grains whole, to avoid waste. In the modern diet, workers transform food in factories before it arrives on grocers' shelves. Processors remove nutritious skins. They cook fruits and vegetables until the original texture and flavor are gone. They strip grains of their most nutritious parts, the germ and the bran.

People's lifestyles and physical activities also changed. Family farms no longer required large numbers of people to do the work. People gradually moved to cities and took less physically demanding jobs in factories and offices. Cars and affordable public transportation ended the need to walk from one place to another. The energy balance began to tip and affect people's ability to manage their weight.

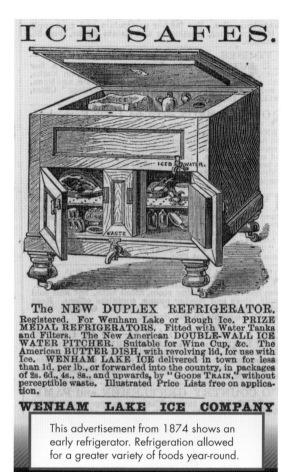

This advertisement from 1874 shows an early refrigerator. Refrigeration allowed for a greater variety of foods year-round.

THE MODERN DIET

Nearly one-quarter of the modern U.S. diet is based on grains such as wheat, oats, and corn. Typically, factories refine grains to make smoother, whiter flour and thickeners. Another 10 percent of U.S. nutrition comes from dairy products such as milk, cheese, and yogurt.

Factories process many other foods and modify them with preservatives, sweeteners, fats, thickeners, stabilizers, and colorings. Consumption of sweeteners has gone from almost none in prehistoric times to more than 150 pounds (68 kg) of various kinds of sugars per person per year. The average American also flavors and preserves foods with more than 21 pounds (9.5 kg) of added salt per year.

Average consumption of vegetable oils has also soared. The average person eats more than 66 pounds (30 kg) of cooking oils, margarine, and shortenings annually. Companies modify many of

A factory employee prepares dough for Wonder Bread. A large part of a modern U.S. diet contains refined grains that have been processed in factories for breads and other foods.

these oils to improve food stability and appearance. Peanut butter manufacturers add oils to their products so they spread easily. But oils naturally separate from the solid ingredients when the peanut butter sits in a jar for days and weeks. So the makers chemically alter the oils to keep the peanut butter mixed well. Margarine is an oily liquid to which manufacturers add chemicals to make it look like butter. These alterations change the way your body processes the oils. These substances can increase blood cholesterol levels and the risk of heart disease and stroke. (A stroke is a sudden, life-threatening lack of oxygen to the brain due to a blocked blood vessel.)

Nutritionists are concerned about the modern American diet. They speculate that our bodies aren't built to process altered foods. They also note that eating large amounts of refined foods and junk foods leads people to eat fewer healthy foods, such as fruits and vegetables. At least half the U.S. population fails to meet recommended dietary allowances for several essential vitamins and minerals. Many scientists believe that vitamin and mineral deficiencies contribute to so-called diseases of civilization. These include high blood pressure, stroke, heart disease, osteoporosis (decrease in bone mass leading to fragile bones), diabetes, some cancers, and asthma.

GENETICS AND WEIGHT

Increasingly, scientists believe that genetics, or inherited character-istics, also determine how people manage their weight. Genetics can affect metabolism, the ways in which people store fat, how active they choose to be, and other factors.

Genes are functional units of the chemical compound deoxyri-bonucleic acid, or DNA. Each gene has a fixed location on one of the twenty-three pairs of chromosomes, the threadlike strands of mate-rial in the nucleus of every cell.

Chromosomes and their genes are responsible for passing on hereditary characteristics from one generation to the next during reproduction. The mother and the father each contribute a single set of chromosomal strands with a unique variety of genes. Each gene codes for a specific trait, such as eye color, sex, stature (physical height), or blood type.

PATTERNS OF INHERITANCE

Some traits are determined by a single pair of genes, one contributed by the mother and one by the father. Only the dominant, or stronger gene in the pair, is expressed. The other remains in the background as recessive and inactive. An example of a single-gene, all-or-nothing trait is eye color. Being left- or right-handed is another example.

Many more traits are polygenic. That is, they are under the control of not one but several pairs of genes. The traits may be expressed in a variety of forms, depending on how the parents' genes blend together in the offspring. Stature and skin color are good examples of the many variations possible when polygenic genes from both parents govern results. Researchers think that genes help determine body type and how the body stores and burns fat.

Everyone is born with an estimated five billion fat cells. As babies grow and become children and adolescents, the number and size of the fat cells continue to increase. An adult with a healthy weight has more than thirty billion fat cells. Each of them grows to about four times the size of the fat cells present at birth.

When people gain or lose a modest amount of weight in adulthood, they don't add or subtract fat cells. Rather, the elastic fat cells swell or shrink in size to accommodate the amount of fat droplets squeezed inside. But even fat cells have their physical limits. About the time that a person crosses the line from overweight to obese, the body has to produce additional fat cells to absorb the extra fat globules. In some instances, the body may make more than one hundred billion additional fat cells. Once the body makes additional fat cells, it can't get rid of them. If a person goes on a diet, the fat cells can only shrink in size, not in numbers. The fat cells remain ready—almost eager—to take up fat again if dieters begin eating more calories than they need.

The accumulation and distribution of fat-storage cells varies with age and gender and to some extent genetic inheritance. At about the age of seven, girls start to increase their body fat stores. They continue on this path until about the age of seventeen when their fat stores level off.

Girls with higher-than-average body fat may experience early puberty. Breast development can begin as early as six years old. Menstrual periods can start at age eight or nine. Girls in physically demanding sports will have lower body fat into their teens. Their periods may be delayed until they are fifteen years old. This is about the same age as girls who lived a century ago, when everyone was more active.

Active boys younger than ten years old can have soft, even chubby, bodies. But when boys enter puberty, between ten and twelve, they tend to build more muscle and lean tissue than girls do.

The part genetic inheritance plays can be seen by studying identical twins. Identical twins gain weight at the same rate and in the same physical patterns whether or not they are raised in the same household. But fraternal twins, whose genetic makeup differs somewhat, may not show much similarity in weight gain.

FAT IN ADULTHOOD

By their early twenties, women and men differ in body composition and fat distribution in very noticeable ways. Women's fat—ideally about 25 percent of total body weight—is stored chiefly in their hips, thighs, buttocks, and breasts. This is because of the female's biological role as child bearer. Men's fat—ideally about 15 percent—is

mostly around the abdomen, where it adds a little extra protection for internal organs. When men and women gain excess pounds, they tend to get fatter in these gender-specific ways.

Any extra fat can affect a person's health. But researchers believe that the typical male way of gathering fat around the midsection tends to have more serious consequences than the typical female way. These two profiles are sometimes referred to as the apple (men) and the pear (women). The fat in bulging waistlines and chests of overweight men wraps around vital organs and interferes with the functioning of the heart and the lungs.

The manner in which women carry extra weight does not tend to interfere with organ function. Researchers say that while carrying extra weight is never good for posture or joints, it is less harmful overall when concentrated in the hips and legs. As a general rule, any

Different people have different body shapes and carry extra fat in different ways. Men tend to carry extra fat around the middle. Women carry extra pounds around the hips.

September 1, 2010

'Fat genes' don't mean fat jeans
Exercise overrides heredity

If you've been blaming your weight on your genes, get out and take a brisk walk. It will help fight your tendency toward overweight, a new study shows.

Researchers in Great Britain studied 12 genetic variants known to increase the risk of obesity and tracked the physical activity levels of 20,430 people.

They created a genetic summary score to quantify a person's risk of obesity and then examined whether an active life could reduce the genetic influence.

They found that physical activity can reduce the genetic tendency toward obesity by 40%.

"Our findings challenge the popular myth that obesity is unavoidable if it runs in the family," says senior researcher Ruth Loos of Great Britain's Medical Research Council in Cambridge. "We see this as a hopeful message."

You can get the benefits without running marathons, she says. You can walk the dog, bike to work or take the stairs: "Being active about 30 minutes a day is a good start in reducing the effects of the genes."

U.S. experts say the study adds to the data on the importance of exercise for weight control. "This is more evidence that behavior can modify genetic predisposition," says Tim Church, director of preventive medicine research at the Pennington Biomedical Research Center in Baton Rouge.

John Jakicic, director of the Physical Activity and Weight Management Research Center at the University of Pittsburgh [Pennsylvania], agrees.

"Just because someone has the genes does not mean that they will become overweight or obese," he says. "Lifestyle such as physical activity can modify the effect."

—*Nanci Hellmich*

woman of average height (about 5 feet 4 inches [1.6 meters]) with a waistline of 35 inches (89 centimeters) or greater is at health risk, regardless of her BMI. Similarly, a man with a waistline of 40 inches (102 cm) or more is at risk.

OTHER FACTORS AFFECTING BODY WEIGHT

When it comes to managing weight, however, genes are not destiny. Genes simply create a person's tendency to being overweight or underweight or average. This makes it easier for some people to stay at a healthy weight than others. But the main cause of modern obesity is the collision between the body's ancient means to survive in times of famine and the Western lifestyle of excess.

Modern food is tasty, convenient, moderately priced, and almost always available. That makes the experience of eating more like recreation than survival for many people. Americans also spend more time than ever before in sedentary pursuits—sitting at a desk, watching TV, surfing the Internet, playing video games, and driving. This all adds up to greater caloric intake than output. It also leads to weight gain, even among young children.

Urban density is another contributing factor. More and more people leave rural communities to live closer together in bigger buildings and larger suburbs and cities. They have fewer safe places to walk, jog, and enjoy the activities that promote fitness.

And schools are cutting back on physical education programs. Most public schools do not provide what physical education advocates recommend for healthy physical development—gym classes five times a week. And in places where school budgets are tight, physical education is often one of the first programs cut entirely. That leaves many students living in cities and suburbs with few chances to exercise.

People also must deal with psychological and emotional factors linked with obesity. For some people, overeating has become an easy distraction from negative emotions such as boredom, sadness, loneliness, or anger. Recent studies show that eating foods high in fat and sugar calms nerves and relieves stress, if only for a short while. That may explain why so many people in stressful modern society

In the twenty-first century, many schools do not offer gym class. Lack of exercise is a big reason that people gain weight.

seem driven to eat junk food. Eating also has profound psychological links to parental love. Nurturing parents are the first to feed us and to worry over us. For this reason, eating often carries memories of security.

Food is also a form of self-medication for people suffering from seasonal affective disorder (SAD). This condition is linked to fewer hours of sunlight and longer hours of darkness in winter. People with SAD report that they are driven to eat more and sleep to excess. And researchers have linked sleep deprivation (anything less than seven to nine hours within each twenty-four-hour cycle) to increased cravings for candy, sweets, and salty snacks.

CHAPTER THREE

THE SUPERSIZE HABIT

CONSTANZA'S STORY

When Alicia Stepic looks at her little sister, she has mixed feelings. Constanza is smart and pretty, and she's overweight. She already weighs 20 pounds (9 kg) more than Alicia does.

Alicia is happy that her sister doesn't have the hard life she had growing up before the family emigrated from Serbia to the United States. She remembers that it was rare to leave the dinner table with a full stomach, except maybe on holidays. And everyone in their town traveled on foot or by bicycle—buses and cars were rare. Alicia recalls that everyday life was active, with everyone working hard. Young people pitched in at family farms and shops when they weren't at school.

Everything is different in the United States. The Stepics enjoy many features of middle-class life, including plenty of food and leisure time. Like many American kids, Constanza spends much of her after-school time snacking in front of the TV, talking on the phone, and playing video games. On weekends they go on outings to parks or museums. But the part Constanza likes best is the fast-food restaurants.

Alicia is concerned. She reads the newspapers. She knows that if her sister's weight gain continues at its current rate, she is almost certainly headed for health problems in adulthood—maybe even sooner. Alicia wishes she could get Constanza to adopt healthier habits—maybe to stop eating so much fast food or even play an after-school sport that would get her moving more and sitting less. But Constanza isn't interested.

How many times have you eaten at a restaurant and taken home leftovers because you couldn't finish your meal? Americans live in a "supersize" culture. In recent years, the size of U.S. dinner plates has grown a great deal. According to the food-service industry, the diameter of the average restaurant dinner plate has increased from 10 inches (25 cm) to 14 inches (35 cm). Many cereal bowls and drinking cups have also grown, all in the name of "bigger is better."

Food portions to fill these plates have grown accordingly, along with the numbers of calories they represent. Nutrition researchers estimate that since the mid-1980s, the increase in average portion sizes has caused the average American's caloric intake to go up about 150 calories a day. That works out to an extra 1,050 calories a week and 54,600 calories a year. Since a pound (0.5 kg) of fat equals 3,500 calories, people can easily gain up to 15 pounds (7 kg) a year.

USA TODAY Snapshots®

How many times a week do you choose fast food as a dining option for your family?

1-3 times a week **63.2%**

3-5 times a week **3.0%**

Never **33.8%**

Source: Market Day survey of 600 mothers of school-age children

By Michelle Healy and Sam Ward, USA TODAY, 2009

PORTIONS AND SERVINGS

To get a better handle on the sneaky effects of overeating, we have to begin with a brief description of what portion size and serving size really mean. Though you might think they are the same, portions and servings rarely are. Portion size describes the actual quantity of food on your plate. It's whatever you or the person spooning out the food decides to make it. Serving size is a scientific unit of measure.

It's a fixed amount based on what nutritionists believe are the needs of the average person.

More often than not, portions are much larger than serving sizes. They're getting bigger every year. It's very hard to know how many calories you are eating unless you carry around a measuring cup, a food scale, and a pocket calculator. Most people, it turns out, underestimate what they consume by about 25 percent.

Food packagers only make it harder. To help packaged foods appear to have fewer calories than they actually do, package label information is often way out of whack with the way people eat those foods. For example, most potato chip packages show nutrition facts based on a 1-ounce (28 g) serving (about fifteen chips). But most people eat a lot more than that in a sitting. People must read labels very carefully to determine the actual calories in the portion they eat.

Government nutritionists developed the concept of serving size as part of a broader program to help Americans adopt a varied, healthful diet. You are probably familiar with the U.S. Department of Agriculture's (USDA) food pyramid, introduced in 1991. The original pyramid depicted the basic food groups within a triangular chart. The largest segment, at the base, was grains; followed by fruits and vegetables; dairy products, meats, and other proteins; and fats and sweets at the top, with an instruction to "use sparingly." In 2005 the USDA did away with the original design and introduced MyPyramid.gov, an interactive website that provides dietary guidelines and personalized plans for weight loss. In 2010 the USDA and the Department of Health and Human Services announced Dietary Guidelines for Americans (dietaryguidelines.gov). These guidelines are meant to promote health, reduce the risk of disease, and reduce obesity rates nationwide.

But try as the USDA and others have, most people continue to think portions when they read servings. We've all heard the expression "his eyes are bigger than his stomach." This means that people take more food than they can handle. It's not just a saying, however. Experiments have shown that many people have a hard time matching their eating habits to their eating needs.

Most people develop their sense of reasonable portion sizes based on what they are taught at home. American parents tend to serve generous portions of food to their children and then urge them to clean their plates. And children usually eat what is put in front of them, regardless of how hungry they are. These habits can be very hard to break. And over time, they make it difficult for people to be aware of their own natural hunger and satiety signals.

Larger portions aren't always more expensive. The small meal at left is actually more expensive than the large meal at right. But the extra calories in the large meal may be more than is healthy.

McDonald's

Quarter Pounder w/Cheese
"Small" Meal
$4.40
890 cal

Quarter Pounder w/Cheese
Large Extra Value Meal
$4.32
1,380 cal

8 extra cents → 490 *fewer* calories

USA TODAY.
HEALTH REPORTS:
DISEASES AND DISORDERS

NUTRITION LABELS

In 1990 the Food and Drug Administration (FDA) started requiring food manufacturers to include nutrition information on all packaged foods. Nutrition Facts and other data disclose the product's nutritional value and ingredients. Consumers can use the labels to help choose what foods to eat and how much is appropriate for a healthy diet. Under Nutrition Facts, look for three key sections: serving information, calorie information, and percent of daily value.

The serving size indicates the amount of product that the nutrition information on the label represents. The "servings per container" tells you how many of those servings are in an entire box, bag, can, or bottle. Pay close attention to both numbers. For example, if a potato-chip manufacturer bases all the label information on a 1-ounce (28 g) serving size—about fifteen potato chips—and you eat the whole 7-ounce (198 g) bag, you have to multiply all the other label information by seven.

If you're trying to cut down on the amount of fat you consume, the number of "calories from fat" is especially important. A 1-cup serving of packaged macaroni and cheese contains 250 calories in total. But it is very high in fat. About half the total calories come from fat. So the label shows 125 calories from fat.

The "% Daily Value" indicates the nutrients in one serving. For example, if the label lists 15 percent calcium, it means that one serving provides 15 percent of the calcium you need

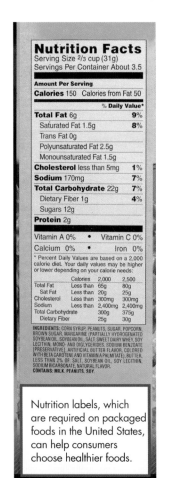

Nutrition labels, which are required on packaged foods in the United States, can help consumers choose healthier foods.

each day. In general, nutritionists consider foods with 5 percent or less of a nutrient to be low in that nutrient. Twenty percent or more is high. People should choose foods high in vitamins, minerals, and fiber, and low in fat, cholesterol and sodium.

Food labels also list the ingredients in the product. They are listed in order of quantity, with the largest at the top. Be aware that manufacturers use chemical names you may not recognize. Fructose, sucrose, glucose, and corn syrup are all sugars. Manufacturers often list these separately, so you have to add all the sugars together to get the full picture. Sodium chloride is the chemical name for table salt.

Packaging may also include one or more descriptive terms such as "sugar free" or "high fiber." Once people started paying attention to nutrition labels, food manufacturers started using nutritional claims as marketing tools. They would put misleading information on packages to entice nutrition-conscious consumers to purchase their

After more consumers started paying attention to nutrition labels, food manufacturers put positive nutrition information on the front of their products to help sell them.

www.usatoday.com

Money
SECTION B

January 25, 2011

From the Pages of USA TODAY

Food labels go to front of packages

Grocery shoppers will soon see the amount of calories, salt, sugar and saturated fat per serving plastered on the front of many popular food and beverage packages.

The food industry unveiled its voluntary front-of-pack labeling, called Nutrition Keys, designed to help make healthful choices.

The Nutrition Keys also can include up to two other nutrients, such as potassium, fiber, vitamin A, vitamin C, vitamin D, calcium, iron or protein.

The program is designed to "promote healthier lifestyles," says Pamela Bailey, president of the Grocery Manufacturers Association, which announced the program with the Food Marketing Institute.

Consumers will start seeing the labels on some food packages in the next few months, but they won't be widely found until the end of the year. The program applies to packaged foods, but not fresh foods such as individual bananas or apples.

The plan is already drawing fire from some critics who say the industry is trying a pre-emptive strike so it won't have to use a plan being developed by the Food and Drug Administration.

"Just putting those numbers on the front of packages could be confusing rather than helpful," says Kelly Brownell, director of the Rudd Center for Food Policy and Obesity at Yale University. "People may not know how to use these numbers in the context of a day's diet."

brand. But then the FDA established standards for using terms such as "low fat" or "high fiber." For example, a product must contain 40 calories or fewer per serving to be called "low calorie."

TRENDS IN AMERICAN EATING HABITS

Americans' growing taste for sweet foods contributes to the national weight gain. We are all born with a preference for sweets. But how

The program has not been tested or approved by an impartial group and doesn't contain a simple color-coding system that would help consumers make sense of the numbers, he says.

Marion Nestle, professor of nutrition at New York University and author of *Food Politics*, says, "It's hard not to be outraged at industry pre-emption of what FDA is trying so hard to do."

But Bailey says that last March, first lady Michelle Obama challenged the industry to develop a front-of-pack labeling system to help busy consumers make informed decisions.

The White House issued a statement recognizing the companies "for the leadership they have shown in advancing this initiative" but stating that the FDA "plans to monitor this initiative closely and will work with experts . . .

to evaluate whether the label is meeting the needs of American consumers and pursue improvements as needed."

The government asked the Institute of Medicine (IOM) to come up with ideas for front-of-package labeling. The report on the first phase of that study is out, and the second phase will be released in the fall. The FDA has been reviewing the IOM report and conducting other research.

—*Nanci Hellmich*

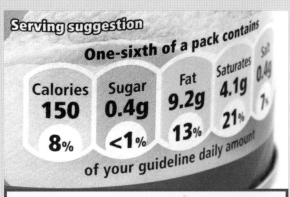

This close-up shows the nutrition information on the front of a can of food.

much is OK? The USDA says a healthy diet should include no more than 10 teaspoons (40 g) of sugar per day, roughly the amount found in one 12-ounce (355 ml) soft drink. But by a recent USDA estimate, the average American consumes about 34 teaspoons (136 g) daily.

Sweeteners are not only in desserts and candy bars, but in cereals, ketchup, juice drinks, pickles, yogurt, canned soups, spaghetti sauce, and peanut butter. Estimates indicate that in the United States, the intake of sugars has increased nearly 30 percent since the early 1980s.

The rise in America's intake of sweets is closely linked with developments in the availability of low-cost sweeteners. In the 1970s, the U.S. Department of Agriculture began giving farmers financial assistance to plant corn. The goal was to produce cheap ingredients for the food industry. The industry was rapidly growing as it mass-produced convenient foods for a growing middle class. In almost no time, the country had excess corn crops. Food scientists began searching for new ways to use it. Soon, scientists in Japan developed high fructose corn syrup (HFCS). Food producers prefer HFCS to other sweeteners because it is extremely cheap to manufacture. It is intensely sweet, so a little bit goes a long way.

The adoption of HFCS had a positive effect on food manufacturers' profits. But many nutritionists believe it has had a negative effect on the health of Americans. When the body digests glucose, the sugar found in carbohydrates, the body produces the hormone leptin. This hormone turns off the hunger signal and decreases appetite. Fructose bypasses this and other digestive controls in ways that encourage greater storage of fat. Since the 1970s, when scientists introduced HFCS, the consumption of corn sweeteners has gone up more than 400 percent. Many scientists believe that the rise in obesity is not just coincidence. They believe it is a direct effect of the widespread use of HFCS. Others think that it is not any more harmful than ordinary white sugar.

The American Heart Association recommends that most women should consume no more than 100 calories a day from added sugar from *any* source. Men should consume no more than 150 calories a day from added sugar. That's about 6 teaspoons of added sugar per day for women and 9 teaspoons for men. Here are some ways to cut back on sugar consumption:

- Avoid sugary, nondiet sodas. Drink water or other unsweetened beverages instead.

- Choose breakfast cereals carefully. Avoid nonnutritious and sugary, frosted cereals.
- Eat fewer processed and packaged foods, such as baked goods and cookies and cakes. Even some microwaveable meals contain excessive amounts of sugar. Be sure to check the Nutrition Facts.
- Snack on vegetables, fruit, low-fat cheese, whole-grain crackers, and low-fat yogurt instead of candy, pastries, and ice cream.

Drinking sugary soda is one of the ways people consume a large number of calories quickly.

SNACK ATTACK

High-fat, calorie-dense junk food is everywhere. Vending machines are in school corridors and cafeterias, and at gas stations and playgrounds. Junk foods fill up more shelf space in many supermarkets than do nutrient-rich foods such as fruits, vegetables, fish, and meat.

Food companies may introduce as many as three thousand new candies, desserts, ice creams, and snacks in a single year. And advertising on TV, movie screens, the Internet, and in magazines and newspapers influences our food choices.

Many food suppliers (including Burger King, Coca-Cola, McDonald's, and Pepsi) have started taking new approaches to promoting their products. They place advertisements in video games and text messages. They place products in blockbuster movies, sporting events, and educational sponsorships. They also engage in a practice called buzz. They hire teenagers who talk up specific products among their friends. In exchange, the teenagers receive discount coupons and other bonuses.

Investments in marketing certainly pay off. Studies show that children begin to be aware of brand names by the time they are two years old. By three, many of them also make what psychologists call an emotional connection with particular brands—that eating certain brand-name foods makes them strong, cool, or smart. By the time the same kids reach first grade, they view perhaps ten thousand food advertisements a year. They develop strong brand loyalty

The Coca-Cola glasses aren't on the *American Idol* set because judges *(from left)* Steven Tyler, Jennifer Lopez, and Randy Jackson put them there. The cups are there because the Coca-Cola Company paid for them to be there.

to certain cereals, candies, and soft drinks. Costly as these advertising campaigns are, advertisers know that children will eventually become adult purchasers. Many of them carry their early food preferences with them.

The many billions of dollars spent on advertising packaged snack foods also overwhelm publicly sponsored efforts to promote healthier eating. The CDC's "Fruit and Veggies— More Matters" fruit-and-vegetable campaign, for example, cannot compete when it has an annual budget of less than $5 million. And the National Milk Processor Board's "Got Milk" campaign struggles against brilliantly staged soft drink ads.

Members of the cast of *Modern Family* appear in a "Got Milk" ad in 2011. The amount spent on campaigns for healthy products such as milk is much less than what is spent on ads for soft drinks.

OUT OF THE KITCHEN

Americans eat fewer meals at home than they once did. Adults work long hours away from home. Their children's schedules are busier than ever. Fast-food restaurants are very effective at promoting the convenience and dollar value of their offerings. All of these factors add to the decline in home-cooked meals. Annual sales of fast food in the United States have grown from about $6 billion in the late 1970s to more than $140 billion in the twenty-first century.

www.usatoday.com

USA TODAY

News

SECTION A

September 24, 2010

From the Pages of USA TODAY

Study: USA is fattest among advanced countries

The United States is the fattest nation among 33 countries with advanced economies, according to a report from an international think tank.

Two-thirds of people in this country are overweight or obese; about a third of adults—more than 72 million—are obese, which is roughly 30 pounds [14 kg] over a healthy weight.

Obesity rates have skyrocketed since the 1980s in almost all the countries where long-term data is available, says the report from the Organization for Economic Cooperation and Development (OECD), which works on policies to promote better economies and quality of life. Countries with the fastest obesity growth rates are the United States, Australia and England.

"Obesity is a growing threat to public health in all the advanced countries throughout the world," OECD spokesman Matthias Rumpf says. Obesity causes illnesses, reduces life expectancy and increases health care costs, he says.

Obesity increases the risk of heart disease, diabetes, several types of cancer and

The move toward eating out comes with a big health cost. Compared to home-cooked meals, most food at fast-food restaurants has more fat, more sugar, more salt, and fewer of the kinds of nutrients that a healthy body needs. Scientists have little doubt that Americans' unhealthy diet is closely connected to the popularity of fast food.

Because of this, state and federal regulators have become more involved in finding solutions to obesity. Consumer-interest groups recognized that health issues related to being overweight led to high health-care costs. They suggested that fast-food companies should be made financially accountable for the low nutritional quality of other diseases. Obesity costs the U.S. an estimated $147 billion in weight-related medical bills in 2008, according to a study by government scientists.

"We have to find the most effective and cost-efficient way to deal with the problem," Rumpf says. "Countries can learn from each other, and the best and most effective policies can be used in all countries."

Among OECD's recommendations:

Individual lifestyle counseling by family doctors and dietitians to increase the life expectancy and quality of life for people who are obese or at risk of becoming so. "It costs a lot of money," Rumpf says, "but you get a lot for this money."

Health-promotion campaigns, compulsory food labeling and a serious commitment from the food industry to stop advertising unhealthy foods to kids.

"There are a lot of these things going on in the U.S. already, but the question is (whether) you can adjust and redirect the policies to make them more effective," he says. "No one can fix the problem, but we can reduce it."

Neville Rigby, director of the European Obesity Forum, says the OECD report "is important because it provides clear evidence that the way most countries have been approaching obesity has been doomed to failure."

"Obesity must be tackled by a multi-pronged approach that involves a combination of strong policy measures at the same time as individual management issues are addressed by physicians and their teams," he says.

The report "makes the case for a much more robust set of government and societal actions," Rigby says. If society waits for business and individuals to do what is really needed, "the obesity epidemic will simply get much, much worse."

—Nanci Hellmich

their offerings. Tobacco companies had been held liable in the same way for the health damages caused by smoking.

But fast-food restaurants and snack-food packagers and their lobbyists (the professionals who work to influence government officials on behalf of their clients) launched a major counterattack. This resulted in "common sense consumption" laws. Voters in more than thirty states have passed public laws that stop people from suing food companies for causing obesity or any other diseases.

Since 2000 a number of government-sponsored programs have attempted to combat the obesity epidemic. In 2004 the then governor of Arkansas, Mike Huckabee, launched the "Healthy Arkansas"

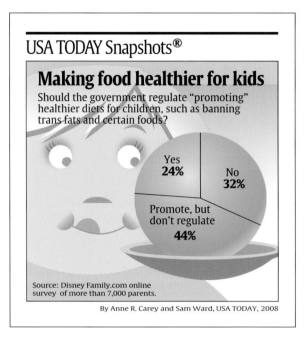

USA TODAY Snapshots®

Making food healthier for kids

Should the government regulate "promoting" healthier diets for children, such as banning trans fats and certain foods?

Yes **24%**

No **32%**

Promote, but don't regulate **44%**

Source: Disney Family.com online survey of more than 7,000 parents.

By Anne R. Carey and Sam Ward, USA TODAY, 2008

plan to improve his state's poor health and obesity scores. Huckabee described his home state as "the land of the deep fried." He showed he meant business by shedding more than 100 pounds (45 kg) himself. He also set up a number of positive health programs in the state. Several of them reward healthier eating and exercise habits among Arkansas's schoolchildren. The U.S. government continues to develop programs to help citizens adopt a healthy lifestyle. The USDA's MyPyramid Ten Tips Nutrition Education series provides tips on decreasing salt intake, eating more whole grains, and cutting back on sweets.

Some local officials also push for healthier citywide food programs. In 2006 the New York City Board of Health voted to ban trans fats (unsaturated fats that increase LDL levels) at restaurants and bakeries. The board also passed a measure that required restaurants to include calorie content information on their menus. These health and weight policies focus on changing individual habits and giving people tools to help them make healthy choices.

FIGHTING THE TREND

Learning to recognize a healthy portion size and understanding your body's nutrition needs are essential to a healthful, satisfying diet. While you might not be able to have the food pyramid at your fingertips at all times, you can follow these tips for healthier eating habits:

- Snack from a plate, not from the bag. Put out a healthy amount of snack food and then stick to that amount.
- Don't rush meals. Sit down and eat slowly, tasting each bite. Use the time to enjoy friends and family too. Remember that it takes about twenty minutes for the brain to get a signal that the stomach is full.
- Avoid some or all the special toppings (cheese, special sauce, bacon, etc.) on burgers and pizzas. They add a lot of fat, sugar, salt, and calories.
- Don't get trapped by the "value" idea into buying the larger sizes. There's no value in eating more food than the body needs.
- Use the "doggy bag strategy," saving half of a portion for another meal if you get an overly large portion. Or share the meal with a friend.
- Don't drink soda every time you're thirsty. Nothing quenches thirst better than water. Water has no calories.
- Know your BMI. If you are moving toward the unhealthy range, take steps to adopt healthier habits.
- Exercise. If you're not certain how much exercise is good for you, ask your doctor. Whatever your weight and eating habits, being physically active is always great for your health.

CHAPTER FOUR

YOUR WEIGHT AND YOUR HEALTH

JESSICA'S AND LEO'S STORIES

Jessica Loos recalls that her battle with weight began when she was in kindergarten. She had a difficult relationship with her parents, was often depressed, and used food to fill the void in her life. At twelve she began the first of fifty serious attempts to lose weight by dieting. Every attempt ended in failure, often with a climactic episode of binge eating.

By the time Jessica graduated from high school, she weighed more than 200 pounds (91 kg). "Once you lose control like that, eating and gaining become habitual, like an addiction," she observes. At twenty-six, she weighed 323 pounds (147 kg) and was unable to get a good job. Despite her youth, her health deteriorated quickly. She had regular bouts of back pain, skin infections, and poor circulation. Jessica's doctor told her that she was at risk for diabetes.

Leo Loos, her husband, was also morbidly obese. Relatively trim as a teenager, Leo started gaining weight rapidly at twenty when he came home from the army. Without any immediate goals to motivate him, Leo took to watching TV and eating junk food all day. He quickly gained 70 pounds (32 kg). Though he eventually found a job he liked, his unhealthy eating habits stayed with him, and his body swelled to 387 pounds (176 kg). At thirty Leo had back pain, skin disorders, sleep apnea, gallstones, and high blood pressure.

The Looses' problems with weight are by no means unusual. A 2009 study by the CDC found that health-care costs related to obesity were as high as $147 billion in one year. And obese patients spent an average of $1,429 more per year for medical care than people of a healthy weight.

Excess weight is a major contributor to every one of the leading causes of preventable death in the United States. These causes include heart disease, diabetes, hypertension, stroke, and certain types of cancer.

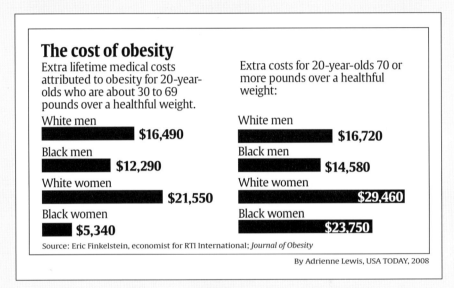

The cost of obesity

Extra lifetime medical costs attributed to obesity for 20-year-olds who are about 30 to 69 pounds over a healthful weight.

White men
$16,490

Black men
$12,290

White women
$21,550

Black women
$5,340

Extra costs for 20-year-olds 70 or more pounds over a healthful weight:

White men
$16,720

Black men
$14,580

White women
$29,460

Black women
$23,750

Source: Eric Finkelstein, economist for RTI International; *Journal of Obesity*

By Adrienne Lewis, USA TODAY, 2008

HEART DISEASE

Heart disease is the leading cause of death in the United States. It sometimes begins in childhood, particularly among children who are in the highest percentiles of weight for their age. But the effects are subtle and the young body is relatively resilient. Doctors may not detect the damage for many years. A much larger population develops heart disease in adult life. An unhealthy diet leading to increased weight and obesity is a major risk factor.

The relationship between excess weight and heart disease is fairly direct. Consider first the burden placed upon the arteries, which make up a major part of the body's blood transport system. The arteries carry oxygenated blood from the heart to every part of the body. To do this, they have thick, muscular walls that expand to accommodate the blood surging through them each time the heart beats.

From birth, your arteries work hard twenty-four hours a day, 365 days a year, even when you are physically fit. They are put under greater stress when they have to pump blood throughout a system whose "plumbing" is becoming more clogged and less flexible. One result is a condition known as high blood pressure.

Blood pressure is the force of blood against the arterial walls. A nurse or a doctor measures your blood pressure by placing an inflatable pressure cuff on your upper arm over the artery. The cuff measures two things: the pressure the blood exerts on arterial walls when the heart contracts (systolic pressure) and the force exerted

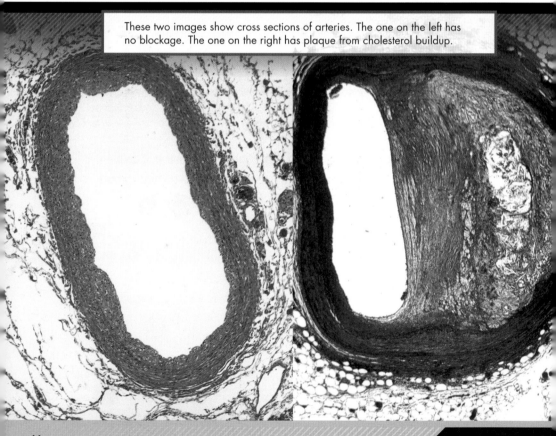

These two images show cross sections of arteries. The one on the left has no blockage. The one on the right has plaque from cholesterol buildup.

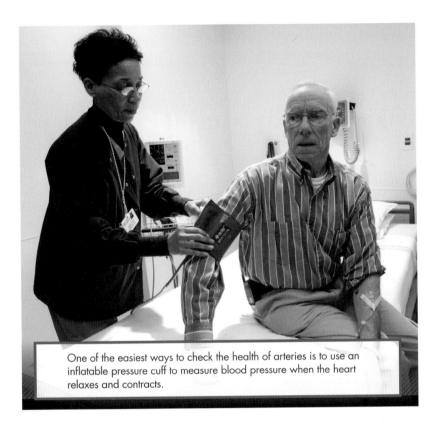

One of the easiest ways to check the health of arteries is to use an inflatable pressure cuff to measure blood pressure when the heart relaxes and contracts.

as the heart relaxes between beats (diastolic). The measurement is given as two numbers: systolic pressure/diastolic pressure. The best blood pressure for an adult is 120/80. Hypertension, or high blood pressure, means pressures are regularly higher than 120/80.

Everyone has temporary spikes in blood pressure when playing sports, doing heavy physical labor, or even just feeling excited. In all these situations, the lungs expand faster to bring in more oxygen. The heart beats faster to carry the oxygen where it's needed. But doctors are most interested in knowing what our blood pressure is when we are sitting still and under no strain. When "resting" blood pressure is higher than 120/80, it signals a problem with the circulatory system.

www.usatoday.com

USA TODAY

News

SECTION A

January 26, 2011

From the Pages of USA TODAY

Smoking, obesity trim life expectancy

Smoking, a declining habit, and obesity, a burgeoning [growing] problem, have cut three to four years off the increasing life expectancy of Americans, an international longevity comparison concludes.

Nationwide, men's life expectancy at birth jumped about five years and women's increased about three years from 1980 to 2007.

"That is a lot of people dying needlessly in their 50s," says report panel co-chairman Samuel Preston of the University of Pennsylvania. High costs aside, U.S. screening and treatment of cancer and heart attacks after age 50 match the best medical results elsewhere, Preston says. But "the evidence suggests the U.S. medical system does a poor job of prevention."

Japan has the highest life expectancy from birth: Men live to 79, and women live to 86. That compares with 75.6 for U.S. men and almost 81 for U.S. women. "That is the shortfall, right there, in a nutshell," Preston says.

Among the report findings:

• Smoking leads to about 450,000 early deaths every year, from lung cancer and respiratory ailments.

Scientists at the CDC have tracked many aspects of U.S. health and nutrition since the late 1960s. They note an upward trend in high blood pressure among children. This rise in the number of children with high blood pressure reflects many changes in childhood behaviors. These changes include eating more fat- and salt-filled snack foods, eating larger portions, and getting less physical exercise at home and at school. All of these contribute to weight gain and to high blood pressure.

Other factors that contribute to high blood pressure are excess fat and salt in the diet. A high-fat diet contributes to clogged and less elastic arteries that never fully relax. Excess salt in the

- Obesity triggers "a fifth to a third of the shortfall of (U.S.) life expectancy," linked to diabetes, heart disease and other diseases.
- Lack of health insurance for 50.7 million people nationwide "has increased mortality and reduced life expectancy," resulting in perhaps 45,000 extra deaths yearly.
- Denmark, which has smoking rates that mirror U.S. rates, saw the same lagging life expectancy increase, while France and other European nations made bigger gains.

"This report should be the beginning of an intense effort to try to further understand the reasons for the low life expectancy," says an e-mail from Vladimir Canudas-Romo of the Johns Hopkins School of Public Health in Baltimore [Maryland]. "The U.S. should be among the leaders on this."

"We're still paying the price for the smoking people did decades ago," Preston says. Lung cancer can take two decades to grow, explaining recent increases among women, many of whom started smoking in the 1970s.

Because U.S. smoking rates have declined, from roughly a third of adults to a fifth, over the past three decades, life expectancy should "catch up over the next few decades," says health policy expert Donald Taylor of Duke University [in North Carolina]. Only Canadians smoke less.

Rising obesity rates, from 20% of the population in 1988 to 33% today, might blunt that "catching up," says demographer Susan Stewart of the National Bureau of Economic Research in Cambridge, Mass.

The link between obesity and an early death is less clear than smoking, the report notes. "But obesity clearly plays a role in reducing life expectancy," Preston says.

—Dan Vergano

system causes the body to retain water. This swells the volume of blood. This leads to more arterial pressure as a greater volume of blood moves through the arteries. Two other common behaviors associated with modern life—eating larger portions and exercising less—are direct contributors to increased weight and high blood pressure.

As if high blood pressure were not a serious enough problem, the overworked heart also tends to suffer. Its muscle action becomes slower, weaker, and less efficient over time. Severely obese people are roughly six times as likely to develop heart disease as those who are of average weight.

DIABETES

There are several kinds of diabetes, including type 1 and type 2. Type 1 diabetes often develops in childhood and affects perhaps 5 to 10 percent of the population. Type 2 diabetes, or adult-onset diabetes, is a serious disorder relating to how the body breaks down carbohydrates. In at least 80 percent of cases, people with type 2 diabetes are overweight.

According to the CDC, 21 million Americans suffer from diabetes. About 90 to 95 percent of them have type 2 diabetes. About 41 million others are at risk for diabetes or are prediabetic. The latter group can lessen risk by making changes in diet and increasing exercise. The CDC estimates that one in three children born in the twenty-first century is on the track to developing diabetes later in life.

Normally, after each meal, blood sugar (glucose) levels rise in the bloodstream as a product of digestion. The pancreas (a gland near the stomach) responds by producing the hormone insulin almost immediately. The insulin attaches to the surface of cells. Just like a key unlocks a door, the insulin "unlocks" the cell surface so the glucose can enter the cell. The cell either uses the glucose as energy or stores it.

If a person has type 2 diabetes, the amount of insulin produced is either insufficient to unlock the cells or the cells become resistant to it. Either way, the result is a buildup of sugar in the bloodstream. This causes the body to work harder to produce more insulin. When insulin levels increase, the body signals the kidneys to hold on to fluids. Blood volume and blood pressure also go up.

Researchers believe that the modern habit of nonstop nibbling and the tendency to become overweight have led to the rapid increase of diabetes in recent years. In the past, they explain, people usually ate three meals a day with nothing in between—

no snacks, no coffee breaks, no sugary drinks. In this pattern of eating, the body produced insulin in three short spurts daily and not throughout the day.

In modern times, metabolic mayhem is the rule. With food available all day long, high levels of glucose course through the body's systems almost nonstop. The insulin "switch" is constantly open. Insulin resistance increases, which leads to type 2 diabetes.

Type 2 diabetes develops slowly and can remain undetected for many years. The body will continually and unsuccessfully try to counter its effects by producing more insulin. The first symptoms a person may notice are decreased energy, unusual and constant thirst, and a frequent need to urinate. But by that time, many parts of the body have already begun to break down.

The consequences of type 2 diabetes can be serious. Continuous high blood sugar levels damage blood vessels, nerves, the heart, and the kidneys. Some of the unused sugars build up in the walls of small blood vessels. This causes them to thicken and leak. It also raises the chances of heart failure, stroke, blindness, and neuropathy (loss of sensation, particularly in legs and feet). A weakened immune system, which fights off infection, causes wounds to heal more slowly. The body becomes more vulnerable to other diseases.

People control type 2 diabetes, particularly in the early stages, with diet (fewer sugars and refined starches; more nutritious patterns of eating) and exercise. Exercise helps glucose enter the cells without insulin. If these measures are not successful, doctors prescribe oral medications such as pills. These medications reduce glucose concentrations in the blood and/or boost the action of the naturally produced insulin. If the pills fail to control glucose, patients must inject insulin with a needle one or more times a day.

Diabetes involves tiny fluctuations in chemical levels in the blood. For this reason, people with diabetes have to track their condition closely.

www.usatoday.com

News
SECTION A

October 22, 2010

From the Pages of USA TODAY

Diabetes cases may double by 2050

The future of diabetes in America looks bleak, according to a Centers for Disease Control and Prevention report, with cases projected to double, even triple, by 2050.

According to the report, one in 10 U.S. adults has diabetes now. The prevalence is expected to rise sharply over the next 40 years with as many as one in three having the disease, primarily type 2 diabetes, according to the report, published in the journal *Population Health Metrics*.

"There are some positive reasons why we see prevalence going up. People are living longer with diabetes due to good control of blood sugar and diabetes medications, and we're also diagnosing people earlier now," says Ann Albright, director of the CDC's Division of Diabetes Translation.

A more diverse America—including growing populations of minority groups such as African Americans and Hispanics, who are more at risk for the disease—factors into the increase as well, Albright says. But an increasing number of overweight Americans also is fueling the stark predictions for diabetes, which should be taken seriously, Albright says.

Diabetes is the No. 1 reason for adult blindness, kidney failure and limb amputation, and it's a large contributor to heart attacks and strokes, she says. "It's also now linked to a form of dementia, some forms of cancer and some forms of lung disease. Diabetes impacts so many systems in the body," Albright says.

Programs and policies to prevent obesity and diabetes need to be put in place at every level, says Duke University Medical Center endocrinologist Susan Spratt, who says schools are a good place to start. Healthful food options in schools and daily physical education classes should be a priority, she says.

"Vending machines should not sell sugar soda or candy bars. School fundraisers should not revolve around unhealthy food," says Spratt, who adds that cities need to be pedestrian-friendly, bike-friendly and safe.

A price will be paid if the projections go unheeded, experts say. The CDC estimates the current cost of diabetes at $174 billion annually—$116 billion of which is in direct medical costs.

Previous research has suggested that the financial burden may easily double in the next 20 years, says David Kendall, chief scientific and medical officer of the American Diabetes Association.

"The financial burden is potentially a very, very troublesome one," Kendall says.

"There's a dual message here: prevention where it's feasible, and critical and early intervention for those already diagnosed," he says.

—*Mary Brophy Marcus*

To do this, they test their blood several times a day using a handheld device that detects their blood glucose level. The device contains a needle that pricks a finger to produce a drop of blood, which is placed on a test strip and into a meter. Readings that are either too high or too low indicate that the body is under stress. The person may begin to show symptoms of anxiety, weakness, shakiness, light-headedness, confusion, and even loss of consciousness.

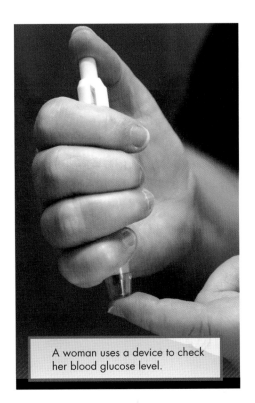

A woman uses a device to check her blood glucose level.

CANCER

Researchers trace the connection between excess weight and cancers to hormones. These substances, which the body produces at high levels in overweight people, speed up the division of cells. Cell division is a necessary part of replacing old cells with new. But when the process speeds up, it can increase the rate at which the body produces cancerous cells. A steady stream of these cells can overwhelm the body's natural immune defenses. If the immune system does not detect and destroy cancerous cells, they remain and form tumors. For example, the female hormone estrogen stimulates the development of breast cancer. Overweight women produce 50 to 100 percent more estrogen than women of average weight. This greatly affects their susceptibility to breast cancer.

Excessive production of the hormone insulin by the pancreas occurs in people with a high BMI. It also happens in people with type 2 diabetes. Doctors believe this explains the increased risk of pancreatic cancer in overweight people.

Excess fat around the abdomen increases the risk of gastric reflux. Reflux occurs when irritating stomach acid bubbles up into the esophagus (the tube running from the back of the mouth to the stomach). Over time this chronic irritation can develop into esophageal cancer.

Malignant (fatal) tumors may avoid detection longer in overweight people than in people of healthy weight. Even with advanced screening devices like mammograms (X-rays of the breasts), tumors are often difficult to find under layers of fat. They often reach a more advanced stage before doctors detect the cancer and begin treatment.

BONE AND JOINT PROBLEMS

Interlocking joints hold the skeletal system together. These joints provide flexibility, stability, support, and protection. Soft cartilage and fluid-filled sacs fill the space in the joints where the bones meet. This way, the joints can move more easily and absorb the shock of running, jumping, walking, bending, and turning. But over time and as a result of constant wear and tear, these cushioning materials lose elasticity. The ends of bones become rough and exposed. Bits of worn bone may fall into the spaces, increasing friction. Every movement becomes more difficult. This condition is osteoarthritis.

Nearly 30 million Americans live with the chronic pain of osteoarthritis (up from 21 million in 1990). While it is not a

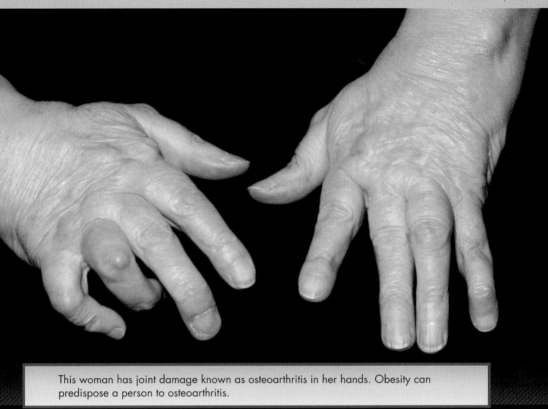

This woman has joint damage known as osteoarthritis in her hands. Obesity can predispose a person to osteoarthritis.

deadly disease, it is a life-changing disability. Many conditions can predispose a person to osteoarthritis. Obesity ranks right at the top. Simply put, heavier people put more stress on the weight-bearing joints of the spine, hips, knees, and ankles, as well as the bones of the feet. The stress increases greatly with even simple movements such as walking. With each additional pound (0.5 kg) above healthy weight, the body exerts two to three times more physical force. So 10 extra pounds (4.5 kg) exerts the force of 30 pounds (14 kg), 20 extra pounds (9 kg) becomes 60 (27 kg), and so on.

Exercise has a positive effect at any weight, but many overweight people are reluctant to exercise. They feel that people may judge them if they exercise in public. Also, exercise is more difficult due to extra weight. The result is that skeletal muscles rarely get the workouts they need to stay strong. Weak muscles, especially in the

www.usatoday.com

Life
SECTION D

January 13, 2010

From the Pages of USA TODAY

At 393 pounds [178 kg], he faced a stark choice

When Tim Wooding, 57, of Wichita, Kansas, decided to lose weight, he had to kick some eating habits that are a nutritionist's worst nightmare.

He was drinking 2 to 4 liters [2.1 to 4.2 quarts] of regular soda a day. At lunch, he'd grab a fast-food double cheeseburger, large fries, large soda and dessert.

He stopped at a convenience store on his way home from work for two big apple fritter doughnuts. And when he got home, he ate a big dinner.

Then, a little more than a year ago, Wooding, a mortgage banker with his own business, went to the doctor, who told him he was on the brink of developing type 2 diabetes. "Although my doctor was talking in medical terms about what I should do, all I could hear was: 'You have two choices: You can live or you can die,'" Wooding says.

"That was a wake-up call for me. I thought if I don't find the time to exercise and watch my eating habits, I will run out of time. All of a sudden, I had plenty of time to exercise."

So he did a complete turnaround on his eating and exercise habits, and in

thighs, make for wobbly walking. This places extra stress on the knees and can lead to osteoarthritis. People with a BMI of 30 to 35 have a much higher risk of osteoarthritis in the knees than people with BMIs of 25 or less. This disability can lead to loss of work and a decline in general health.

Eventually, when the pain and disabilities of osteoarthritis become intolerable, joint-replacement surgery is the only option. A surgeon replaces the diseased joint with artificial bone, or metal, ceramic, or plastic hardware. In overweight people, complications during surgery are more likely and the results are generally poorer.

a year he lost 223 pounds [101 kg]. At 5-foot-8 [1.7 m], he now weighs 170 pounds [77 kg], down from 393 [178 kg].

Wooding researched what he should eat and revamped his diet. He began eating five times a day: a yogurt for breakfast, fruit for a midmorning snack, a salad or sandwich for lunch, an ounce [2 tablespoons] of peanuts as a midaft-ernoon snack, and a low-calorie entree such as Lean Cuisine for dinner. And he began eating more slowly. "Before, I used to inhale food," he says.

During the weight loss, he limited himself to about 1,200 calories a day. Now that he's at his goal weight, he's consum-ing about 1,800 calories or more a day. He allows himself some treats, but there are a few things he won't touch. "I won't ever drink pop again. I won't eat candy and doughnuts."

"I know deep down inside that if I were to allow myself to have an apple fritter or stop at a fast-food restaurant, I could very easily slip back into that kind of eating habit."

Wooding gets up early and goes to the gym daily, where he works out on the elliptical for 30 minutes, walks on the treadmill for half an hour and strength-trains for another 30 minutes. He squeezes in other activities during the day, such as a walk at lunch and using the stairs at work as often as he can.

Before he lost weight, Wooding says it was hard to even get up out of his chair, and he couldn't do the elliptical for more than a minute without getting breathless. "I feel a thousand times better," he says.

He's now healthy, and his blood work indicates he doesn't have diabetes. His ad-vice to others who think they don't have time to make changes: "Don't wait for your doctor to give you some bad news. You don't have the time not to do this."

—Nanci Hellmich

Afterward, rehabilitation is slower. The replacement part is likely to wear out sooner. This can lead to more surgery several years later. Some orthopedic surgeons refuse to perform knee-replacement surgery on people with high BMIs because of the increased complications.

Excess weight can also strain the bones and muscles of the back. Problems with degenerating cartilage or disks in the lower segments of the spine may result. It can also lead to chronic pain caused by pinching of sciatic nerves of the lower back. This pain is often felt down one or both legs.

OTHER DISORDERS

Many overweight people suffer from obstructive sleep apnea. During sleep, their breathing is interrupted repeatedly (apnea) and long enough to decrease the amount of oxygen in the blood and the brain. With each stoppage, the person typically awakes for a split second because the brain senses that levels of carbon dioxide are becoming toxic. It sends an automatic alarm to breathe again.

Risk factors for sleep apnea include excessive weight, a thick neck, and high blood pressure. Overweight people may have fat deposits around the upper airway that can obstruct breathing. A thick neck may cause the airway to narrow. Studies have shown that obstructive sleep apnea is common in people with hypertension, which is also linked with being overweight.

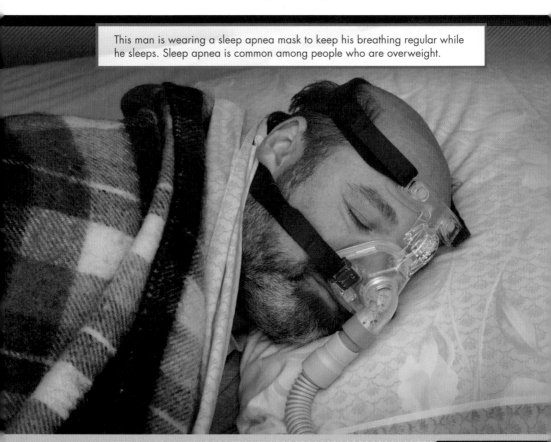

This man is wearing a sleep apnea mask to keep his breathing regular while he sleeps. Sleep apnea is common among people who are overweight.

A person with sleep apnea may be unaware of what is happening for months or years. But the disorder takes a severe long-term toll. The person with apnea awakes exhausted every day, needs to sleep for more hours than normal, and snores very loudly. The person may fall asleep during the day even while driving a car or working a job.

Respiratory insufficiency is a condition in which the lungs decrease in size because of the pressure from excess fat around them. This leads to a decrease in the amount of oxygen going to the muscles and other parts of the body. Respiratory insufficiency causes sufferers to have trouble catching their breath even if they aren't doing much.

Overweight people may also struggle with depression. Studies show that overweight people in the United States face discrimination in all areas of life, from the workplace to dating. Images in the media reinforce the idea that being thin—even unhealthily thin—is the same as being a successful human being. Constant negative challenges to emotions can damage self-esteem. In some instances, this leads to chronic anxiety and depression.

The connection between diseases and obesity are well established. In the majority of cases, people can change the odds in their favor. Even losing a few pounds can make a big difference. The person who commits to a healthy routine of exercise, good nutrition, and gradual weight loss improves his or her chances of living a long, healthy life.

CHAPTER FIVE

THE STRAIGHT SKINNY ON DIETING

TANYA'S STORY

By the time Tanya entered middle school, she was well aware that what her parents referred to as "pleasantly plump" wasn't very pleasant. Some of her classmates had started ridiculing her weight, calling her "whale" to her face. Very unhappy, she tried dieting repeatedly. At first, she would lose some weight, but then she would have a bad day, get discouraged, and begin eating junk food again. As soon as she went off her diet, the weight came back. She thought about exercising but didn't know where to begin. Besides, she wasn't good at sports, and gym class was humiliating. Tanya thought about talking to a doctor or a nutritionist, but dieting never worked anyway, so what was the point? Tanya became depressed, thinking that she was destined to be overweight the rest of her life.

Dieting can be very difficult. The body, once burdened with extra pounds, reprograms itself to hold on to that weight by establishing a new, higher set point. An estimated two-thirds of American dieters regain all the weight they lose within a year. Within five years, 97 percent gain it all back. Many people gain more weight with each cycle, so they end up worse off than they started.

The cycle occurs in part because people are looking for a magic bullet that will solve their problem. A lot of businesses sell the promise of a quick fix. Dieters who follow such plans may lose a lot of weight in the short term. But permanent weight loss requires ongoing, basic changes in habits. These include restricting calorie intake, being selective in choosing foods, and making regular exercise a part of everyday life. Nonetheless, the weight-loss industry is a booming business. In its many forms—books, programs, support groups, liquid diet formulas, and medications—it makes billions of dollars each year selling products and services to Americans who want to lose weight.

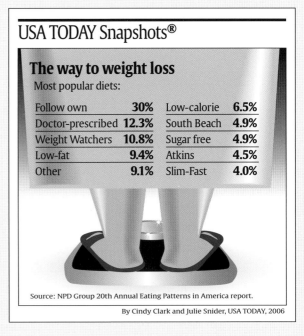

USA TODAY Snapshots®

The way to weight loss

Most popular diets:

Follow own	**30%**	Low-calorie	**6.5%**
Doctor-prescribed	**12.3%**	South Beach	**4.9%**
Weight Watchers	**10.8%**	Sugar free	**4.9%**
Low-fat	**9.4%**	Atkins	**4.5%**
Other	**9.1%**	Slim-Fast	**4.0%**

Source: NPD Group 20th Annual Eating Patterns in America report.

By Cindy Clark and Julie Snider, USA TODAY, 2006

DIET BOOKS AND TV

Do-it-yourself diet books have been around for at least 150 years. A British undertaker named William Banting is usually credited with publishing the first diet book, titled *Letter on Corpulence*, in 1862. In the early twentieth century, Horace Fletcher, another diet wizard, popularized the notion that chewing every bite thirty-two times, once for each tooth, was a surefire way to lose weight. The formerly portly Fletcher came up with this notion after an insurance company claimed he was a poor health risk. They refused to give him a life insurance policy because of his size. People were so taken with the "Chew-Chew Man" that they even gave parties at which a conductor kept time while people chewed in unison. Fletcher was right in one way at least. By slowing down their food consumption, so-called Fletcherizers were able to experience satiety signals before cleaning their plates. This probably helped to discourage excessive eating.

www.usatoday.com

Life
SECTION D

June 16, 2010

From the Pages of USA TODAY

Four steps to fighting obesity

Obesity is "the single greatest threat to public health in this century," an expert panel declared in a report that urges Americans to slash calories and increase their physical activity.

An advisory committee for the 2010 Dietary Guidelines for Americans calls on people to cut back on added sugars and solid fats (butter, marbled meats) and to follow a more nutrient-rich, plant-based diet.

The report is based on the latest scientific evidence and was prepared by a 13-member panel of national nutrition and health experts.

About two-thirds of adults and one-third of children in the United States are overweight or obese. The advisory committee highlighted four major steps:

- Reduce excess weight and obesity by cutting calorie intake and increasing physical activity.
- Shift to a more plant-based diet that emphasizes vegetables, cooked dry beans and peas, fruits, whole grains, nuts and seeds. Increase the intake of seafood and fat-free and low-fat milk and milk products, and eat only moderate amounts of lean meats, poultry and eggs.
- Significantly reduce intake of foods containing added sugars and solid fats, which contribute about 35% of the calories in the American diet. Cut sodium intake gradually to 1,500 milligrams a day and lower intake of refined grains, especially those with added sugar, solid fat and sodium.

John Harvey Kellogg (1852–1943) also contributed to the literature of American dieting. Kellogg was staff physician at a health retreat in Battle Creek, Michigan, and the inventor of the first commercial breakfast cereals. He developed a diet based on roughage, starting with the invention of shredded wheat. The rough cereal was supposed to cleanse the lower intestinal canal. Kellogg also wrote a chewing song to help people trying to diet.

- Meet the 2008 Physical Activity Guidelines for Americans. The Guidelines recommend that adults get at least 2½ hours of moderate-intensity physical activity each week, such as brisk walking, or 1¼ hours of a vigorous-intensity activity, such as jogging or swimming laps, or a combination of the two types. Children and teens should do an hour or more of moderate-intensity to vigorous physical activity each day.

The report calls for many changes in the food environment, including:

- Improve nutrition literacy and cooking skills, and motivate people, especially families with children, to prepare healthy foods at home.
- Improve the availability of affordable fresh produce through greater access to grocery stores, produce trucks and farmers' markets.
- Encourage restaurants and the food industry to offer health-promoting foods that are low in sodium; limited in added sugars, refined grains and solid fats; and served in smaller portions.

The dietary guidelines were first published in 1980 and are updated every five years. They're used for government nutrition programs and education, as well as by dietitians and health professionals to help educate people about eating healthier.

"Basic nutrition advice hasn't changed much over the 30 years that the dietary guidelines have been published, but what has changed is it is harder and harder to eat well," says Margo Wootan, director of nutrition policy at the Center for Science in the Public Interest, a consumer group based in Washington, D.C.

"For Americans today, healthy eating is like swimming upstream. It's not that you can't do it, it's just it's so hard," she says. "Without changing the food environment, people don't stand a chance of following the advice in the dietary guidelines."

Three steps to lower your calories, she says: Cut portions, eat less when dining out and drink fewer sugary beverages.

—*Nanci Hellmich*

A confirmed vegetarian, Kellogg challenged the theories of fellow doctor James H. Salisbury. Salisbury's book, *The Relation of Alimentation and Disease* (1892), argued for the healthful possibilities of ingesting hamburger patties and hot water three times a day. (Dr. Salisbury is the creator of the Salisbury steak.) Dr. William Howard Hay's dietary philosophy included never eating proteins and carbohydrates at the same time.

In 1918 Dr. Lulu Hunt Peters went off in a more scientific direction with the blockbuster title *Diet and Health with Key to the Calories*. She recommended a daily limit of 1,200 calories, which is near starvation. Other book-based diet fads that followed included Christian diets, grapefruit diets, banana and milk diets, lamb chop and pineapple diets, vinegar diets, and foods eaten in "magic pairs."

Two doctors in particular dominated the diet-trend field with strict, low-carbohydrate diets. They advised weight loss through eating more protein and fat. Dr. Robert C. Atkins had not one but three best-selling diet books at the time of his death in April 2003. Then dieters moved on to embrace *The South Beach Diet*, a book by Dr. Arthur Agatston. Experts continue to debate the health effects of these high-protein, low-carbohydrate diets.

A recent development in the dieting craze is the addition of reality TV shows such as *The Biggest Loser*. On the show, contestants compete to lose weight and win a cash prize. Other weight-loss reality shows include *Losing It with Jillian* and *Heavy*. Health experts disagree on whether these shows are a good idea. Some feel that the shows' emphasis on body image can encourage eating disorders and that losing weight as quickly as the contestants do can be risky. Losing too much weight too fast can lead to heart problems and other health issues. At least two contestants on *The Biggest Loser* were hospitalized after collapsing during a race. On the upside, some experts support any show or book that inspires people to change negative behaviors and adopt a healthier lifestyle.

Dr. Arthur Agatston holds two of the popular diet books he wrote in the 2000s.

The Biggest Loser: The Down Side

Contestant Ryan C. Benson lost 122 pounds (55 kg) on the first season of *The Biggest Loser* but gained more than 90 pounds (41 kg) back over the next five years. Doctors generally recommend losing about 2 pounds (0.9 kg) a week, but the average on *Biggest Loser* is 15 pounds (7 kg) a week. Losing weight too quickly and exercising too strenuously when out of shape can weaken the heart. On the first episode of one season, two contestants were hospitalized after a 1-mile (1.6 km) race.

Some contestants drink as little water as possible in the twenty-four hours before a weigh-in to lower their weight. They became dehydrated in the process. Kai Hibbard weighed 144 pounds (65 kg) at the show's finale but then added 31 pounds (14 kg) in two weeks, most of it simply by drinking water. The winners of the first four seasons of the show each gained back at least 20 percent of their total weight at the end of the show. But the show's creators say that at least half of the contestants stay close to their winning weight for several years. They claim that a 50 percent success rate is good enough.

It's important to remember that *The Biggest Loser* is a reality show, a genre that has to be extreme to get people to watch. Doctors constantly monitor the contestants. Needless to say, you shouldn't try the show's methods on your own. Consult your doctor before trying to lose weight. On the road to weight loss and general fitness, slow and steady wins the race.

USA TODAY
HEALTH REPORTS:
DISEASES AND DISORDERS

DIET DEVICES, POTIONS, AND PILLS

Weight-loss devices began to capture the American public's attention after the Civil War (1861–1865). Several approached the problem from an engineering standpoint. For women there was the La Grecque corset. This garment promised to decrease hunger and achieve the look of weight loss by strapping the stomach flat and nipping in the waist to form an hourglass figure. (Fainting from lack of breathing space was a frequent side effect.) For men there was the so-called obesity belt. The belt claimed to zap the overextended belly with jolts of electricity that, over time, would melt fat. Still another solution was a reducing machine, which used two rollers to massage away fat.

Pills both harmless and potent followed these trends. Densmore's Corpulency Cure and Dr. Gordon's Elegant Pills seem to have done no harm other than taking customers' money and leaving them disappointed. These products promised amazing results. They claimed users could indulge in a life of no exercise and overeating with no risk of obesity if they took the product faithfully. People also began using laxatives (drugs used to promote bowel movements) for weight loss in the 1920s. This is a dangerous practice still followed by many people with eating disorders.

DREW'S INIMITABLE "A LA GRECQUE" CORSETS.

This advertisement from the 1890s shows a La Grecque corset. The corset promised to help women lose weight by compressing the waist, which would decrease hunger.

Pharmaceutical companies started promoting the use of amphetamines for weight loss in 1937. By 1970 doctors were prescribing more than two billion amphetamine pills, as appetite suppressants, per year to dieters, some of them children. Amphetamines are stimulants (drugs that stimulate the central nervous system). These drugs expose users to the risks of rapid heart rate, increased blood pressure, dry mouth, hallucinations, seizures, psychosis (a mental disorder), and severe addiction.

In the 1990s, effective diet pills known as fen-phen (a combination of fenfluramine and phentermine) were all the rage. But researchers linked the drug to life-threatening heart-valve problems, short-term memory loss, pulmonary hypertension, and even death. So the FDA withdrew fen-phen from the market in 1997.

Search the Internet for the phrase "diet supplements," and you'll get millions of sites offering dozens of substances. Scientists have found little evidence that any of the over-the-counter pills currently available do anything to effect weight loss. But they do cause side effects that can be troublesome. These include nervousness, irritability, headaches, dry mouth, nausea, constipation, abdominal pain, diarrhea, and sleep problems. Supplements do not have to meet the same high standards of medical testing as prescription drugs. Users often take supplements without any input from their doctor. So any harmful effects and interactions with a user's other medications may not be recognized for months or years.

In addition to pills, liquid diet supplements such as Slim-Fast are widely available. Dieters consume the 220-calorie servings, which come in the form of shakes and bars, in place of two meals each day. The typical problem with these supplements is that users may lose weight briefly. But as soon as they go off the plan, the weight comes back. Diet supplements are big business. Researchers at pharmaceutical companies constantly search for safe and effective prescription drugs that will reduce weight, curb appetite, and burn fat. By some estimates, as many as two hundred experimental drug compounds are in some phase of testing by more than seventy pharmaceutical companies at any time. The company that discovers a safe and effective formula stands to make billions of dollars in profit.

Slim-Fast is a liquid diet supplement. Some people use supplements to lose weight. However, they often have a hard time keeping off the weight after going back to a lifestyle that does not include a healthy diet and regular exercise.

One obstacle to getting these drugs to market is the medical community's fear that they will be used inappropriately by slightly overweight people. The drugs should not be used to shed a few pounds for reasons of appearance only. Exercise and skipping desserts can accomplish this.

LEPTIN

A development that caused quite a stir in the weight-loss industry was Dr. Jeffrey Friedman's 1994 discovery of the hormone leptin. Friedman's research team at Rockefeller University in New York City found that this hormone regulates appetite and weight loss. It also plays a role in blood circulation, the maintenance of body temperature, and the regulation of insulin, among other things.

Leptin releases chemicals that signal the body to stop eating. Many people thought that Friedman had discovered the cure for obesity. They hoped that by artificially increasing leptin levels in overweight people who had low levels of the hormone they would have the "magic bullet" everyone was looking for. But further research has shown that an increase in fat tissue leads to an increase in leptin.

So obese people actually have too much leptin. They have so much that they become resistant to it. This means that their brain does not receive the "stop eating" message.

Even though leptin may not cure obesity, understanding the hormone can help doctors help their overweight patients. Researchers have found that people with high levels of leptin prior to dieting are more likely to regain weight afterward. This information can guide doctors to create specialized weight-loss programs for these patients.

WEIGHT-LOSS PROGRAMS AND DIET DESTINATIONS

Another weight-loss strategy that the diet industry offers is commercial weight-loss plans such as Jenny Craig. Members can enroll at a local weight-loss center or sign up online. The Jenny Craig plan monitors dieters' weight while they eat or drink only certain prescribed foods sold through the plan in restricted amounts. The programs can be expensive, costing almost twice what a typical American spends weekly on food.

Many members report weight loss while they are on these plans. But few people succeed in keeping the weight off for long when the program ends. The most effective plans include support groups and training to change certain behaviors associated with eating. These activities help participants recognize the psychological and practical triggers linked to their overeating. Weight Watchers offers such a program. However, the weekly meeting fee may be more than some people, especially teens, can afford. Overeaters Anonymous is a free group recovery program for compulsive eaters.

A costlier approach to dieting is to attend a diet program at a specialized hospital or health center. Overweight and obese clients enroll at a weight-loss facility. There, programs include medical, nutritional, and psychological counseling; physical rehabilitation;

and even plastic surgery to remove the sagging skin that remains after the fat underneath has been dieted away.

Most people stay at dieting destinations only long enough to achieve their goal of weight loss. Others return for annual tune-ups. A few remain as permanent residents in the larger community. They fear that a return home will put them at risk of gaining the weight back.

Some weight-loss programs are aimed specifically at adolescents and teenagers. Wellspring Academy in California is a residential program that combines schoolwork with analyzing and altering habits that are tied to excess weight gain. The academy allows no smoking, TV, telephone, video games, or other distractions associated with the outside world. Kids wear pedometers (instruments that measure steps taken). They are required to walk a minimum of ten thousand steps per day—a rigorous amount of exercise—to stay in the program. Meals are consistently low in sugar and fat and high in

Wellspring Academy helps students lose weight and learn a healthy lifestyle. Food journals help students monitor their daily calorie intake.

Teens at a camp for overweight children go for a jog to improve their fitness.

healthy nutrition. If all goes as planned, the youngsters return home with a new set of coping skills to deal with future food temptations.

A wide range of summer camps also promise similar guidance to children coping with excess weight and problems of self-esteem. Just being in a place where everyone else is dealing with the same problems can help. But weight-loss camps often lack the facilities, the personnel, and time to promote long-term weight stability or psychological counseling to improve self-esteem. The result is that many campers regain much of the weight they have lost within a few months of returning home.

www.usatoday.com

Life
SECTION D

January 3, 2011

From the Pages of USA TODAY

The biggest burden of them all
When the excuses stop, change can happen

Excuses, excuses, excuses.

Best-selling author Bob Greene, who catapulted to fame as Oprah's personal trainer, has spent years listening to people's reasons for why they don't exercise, lose weight and get healthier. "I have heard every excuse on the planet—except a good one," he says.

Excuses represent a desire to hang on to the life you have now, says Greene, an exercise physiologist and author of a new book, *The Life You Want: Get Motivated, Lose Weight and Be Happy*, written with Anne Kearney-Cooke and Janis Jibrin.

"An excuse is an obstacle that you choose to place in front of yourself. We do it for a variety of reasons, but in general, we do it to justify not changing. When you are out of excuses is when you are ready to change."

Sue Hentschel, 54, of Harrison Township, Michigan, had a good reason for not trying to lose weight and shape up.

Hentschel, co-owner of a dog-grooming business and trained as a licensed practical nurse, had complications from gallbladder surgery in 2001 and had to have several operations to repair the problems. Her doctors told her she shouldn't do strenuous exercise ever again.

"My excuse for being so overweight was that the doctors advised me against exercising, which is what I needed to do to lose excess weight. I ate anything I wanted and didn't exercise," she says. She gained 140 pounds [64 kg] over the next eight years.

Then, in summer 2009, she went to a Detroit Red Wings hockey game with a friend, and she could barely fit into the seat. She told him: "This is the lowest point in my life. I can't even participate in the things I enjoy because of my weight."

That week she vowed to lose weight and start exercising. And Wow, look at her go! Since August 2009, she has lost 146 pounds [66 kg]. At 5 foot 6 [1.7 m], she now weighs 173 [78 kg], down from 319 [145 kg].

Make a choice

People get wrapped up in their own reasons for not losing weight and getting in shape, says Felicia Stoler, a registered dietitian and exercise physiologist in Holmdel, N.J., who works with people to try to trim them down and shape them up. She has written a new book, *Living Skinny in Fat Genes*.

"All I hear are excuses. People offer up excuses because they "don't want to admit why they didn't do something. They can't admit that they just don't feel like doing it," she says.

When clients tell her their reasons for not changing, she shifts the conversation to their choices. "In everything we do, we make choices."

You make a choice about getting up and working out, she says. You make a choice about whether to go to a restaurant that offers healthful options. If you're an emotional eater, you make a choice about whether to turn to comfort food when you're upset, she says.

You make a choice about whether you are eating for your health or just consuming food because it tastes good, Stoler says. "Everything is about making choices, not excuses."

Exercise your options

When it comes to excuses for not exercising or losing weight, lack of time is probably the most common one, trainer Bob Greene says.

People frequently say they don't have time to shop for the right foods, cook healthful meals or exercise. Green doesn't buy any of it. "Not having enough time is not an excuse."

He has studied busy people's schedules, and they all have an hour a day that they are not using efficiently that would be better spent being physically active.

If you can't free up 30, 40 or 60 minutes a day to exercise, you're not valuing your health, Greene says. "When you really break it down, who doesn't have time to care for themselves?"

Another common excuse is what he calls exercise aversion. Even his most famous client, Oprah Winfrey, whom he still works with occasionally, doesn't like to exercise. "I get the question: 'What exercise does she like?' None. There is not one exercise that I can think of."

She has said she doesn't like to exercise but does it because it's good for her, but even then she struggles with consistency, Greene says.

He believes people avoid exercising because they don't want to experience any discomfort from sweating or working hard.

There should not be pain, he says, but discomfort indicates that you're exerting yourself enough to burn calories and improve your health.

There are so many ways to move your body; you need to keep looking until you find what fits, he says. And there are also many ways to distract yourself. Some dedicated exercisers work out while watching their favorite TV show or movie or listening to music. And social people should find a buddy to walk or work out with them.

In making healthful changes in your life, you essentially have to resolve that you haven't lived the life you want to live and you are going to change that.

—*Nanci Hellmich*

THE SURGICAL EXTREME

Surgery for weight loss is the most extreme option. Perhaps the first surgical approach to weight loss was interdental fixation, or jaw wiring. The idea was to wire the upper and lower teeth together in such a way as to prevent the mouth from opening more than half an inch (1.3 cm). This is just enough to make it impossible to chew. The jaw might stay wired for as long as a year while the patient took nourishment from selected liquids and soft foods. It made talking difficult, however, and had many other disadvantages.

Liposuction is another approach, in which fat deposits (sometimes referred to as cellulite) are vacuumed out of specific parts of the body. This is a cosmetic solution and is not intended for removing the large amounts of fat involved in achieving major weight loss. As with any surgery, liposuction has risks of complications, including blood loss, infection, and occasionally death. It is particularly inappropriate for teens and young people, who are still growing.

More drastic surgical approaches include two methods of stomach reduction: gastric bypass surgery, commonly known as stomach stapling, and a banding procedure. In 2006 an estimated 177,000 Americans underwent one form or other of stomach reduction surgery.

Gastric bypass surgery involves shrinking the size of the stomach to a fraction of its original size. People who undergo the surgery will always need close medical supervision. Once done, gastric bypass surgery cannot be reversed.

In gastric bypass surgery, surgeons make an incision in the belly. With surgical staples, they create a pouch big enough to hold perhaps 2 ounces (57 g) of food in the upper part of the stomach. Then they attach a segment of the small intestine to the pouch at the top of the stomach. This allows eaten food to bypass the larger remaining portion of the stomach. The small pouch cannot hold as much food or absorb nearly as many calories as the whole stomach.

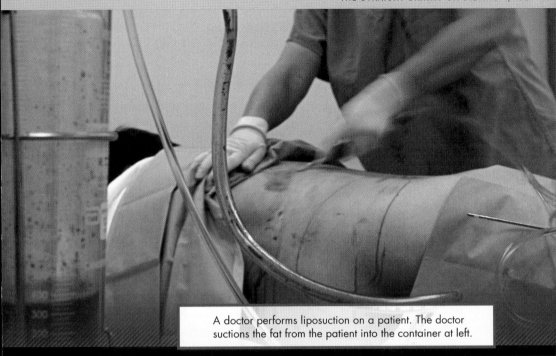

A doctor performs liposuction on a patient. The doctor suctions the fat from the patient into the container at left.

Patients immediately begin to eat less—fewer than 1,200 calories per day. They must eat and drink small amounts frequently and take a collection of vitamins and other essential nutrients to supplement their reduced diets. Patients lose weight quickly. But they risk complications such as blood clots, leaks in the stomach, staples letting go, and internal infection.

Surgical banding is a less expensive procedure, which some doctors claim is safer than gastric bypass. Surgical banding produces more gradual weight loss and can be undone if it is not successful. The surgeon places an adjustable silicone band around the upper part of the stomach. After banding, the stomach can only hold about an ounce (28 g) of food. Periodically, as the patient loses weight, he or she must return to have the band adjusted as necessary. This can be done in the doctor's office, without further surgery. If the doctor and the patient decide that the band is no longer necessary, perhaps because the patient has successfully changed eating behaviors, the doctor can remove the band.

Another method is the intragastric balloon, which has not yet been approved by the FDA for use in the United States. A surgeon inserts a collapsed balloon through a tube in the mouth and guides it down the throat until it reaches the stomach. The surgeon fills the balloon with a sterile liquid, decreasing the stomach's size. The balloon is kept in place for an average of six months while the obese patient adjusts his or her appetite to accommodate the downsized stomach.

Other ideas, such as an implantable stomach pacemaker that tricks the stomach into signaling the brain that it is full, are being tested for medical use. Because obesity is so widespread, researchers spend an increasing amount of time and money to find other high-tech treatments. For people who can't regulate their weight because of genetics or some medical disorder, these high-tech developments may be a solution.

EATING DISORDERS

An eating disorder is a psychological condition that leads to abnormal eating habits involving either insufficient or excessive food intake. Binge eating, or eating large quantities over a short period, may affect as many as 5 percent of obese people. Binge eaters are divided nearly equally among males and females. Some of the symptoms of binge eating are eating with extreme rapidity, eating when not hungry, eating to the point of physical discomfort, and hiding food for eating later when no one can observe. Binges are often triggered by anxiety or stress. Binge eaters feel out of control during an episode and tend to feel guilt and shame afterward.

Anorexia nervosa and bulimia nervosa are disorders that stem from an inappropriate and unreasonable fear of being overweight. People with anorexia go to extreme measures to be thin. This includes self-imposed starvation, sometimes to the point of irreversible organ damage and death. According to the National Institutes of Health, the annual death rate among anorexic females aged fifteen to twenty-four is about twelve times higher than the rate for those who are not anorexic.

People with bulimia alternate repeated episodes of binge eating with self-induced purging, or vomiting. They may also take laxatives, undertake extreme dieting, and exercise rigorously to counteract the effects of bingeing. People with bulimia often manage to maintain near average weight. But they do significant long-term damage to their bodies in the process.

All eating disorders are regarded as unhealthy. For this reason, people who engage in them tend to be very secretive, restricting their behavior to private moments. Even close friends and family may be unaware of what is happening until serious health consequences force others to notice.

Binge eaters usually hide the amount of food they eat and the frequency of their binges.

Eating disorders are also associated with clinical depression, anxiety disorders, and substance abuse. Intervention typically requires a team approach. A medical doctor, a licensed psychiatrist or psychologist, and a nutritional counselor all take part to help the patient change thoughts and behaviors. If you or someone you know has an eating disorder, talk to your parent, your doctor, or another adult you trust about how to get help.

LIFELONG HABITS — THE BEST ALTERNATIVE

Lifelong health habits begin in childhood. Adolescence—when most people start to make their own life choices—is a good time to form healthy eating and exercise routines. Remember first that achieving healthy habits all comes down to a balancing act. The energy you take in through your food should match the energy you expend through basic body functions and physical activity. And how do you achieve that balance? Nutritionists agree that dieting or any other short-term change in your eating habits is rarely effective. The key to getting and staying fit is adopting healthy eating and regular exercising habits that you can maintain year after year.

Here are some basic recommendations that will help improve your health and energy levels, no matter what you weigh:

- Become familiar with the names and benefits of each major food group—grains, vegetables, fruits, milk and milk products, meats and beans, and oils and fats.
- Eat five to nine servings each day of fruits and vegetables. The brighter and more colorful ones are usually more nutritious.
- Pay attention to how much you eat. This means watching serving sizes, eating slowly so that your body has time to tell when you've had enough, and cutting down on unhealthy snacks.

- Choose nutrient-dense foods such as whole grains that have few or no empty calories.
- Consume plenty of fat-free or low-fat milk or equivalent products (yogurt, cheese, etc.) daily for strong bone growth. Recommendations for boys and girls between nine and eighteen years old are three 8-ounce (227 g) portions daily.
- Choose lean, low-fat, and fat-free foods in place of those with saturated fat and trans-fatty acids.
- Educate yourself on the pluses and minuses of salt and sugar. If you're eating lots of processed foods (store-bought prepared foods in cans, bottles, and other packages), you are almost certainly eating too much of both.
- Learn how to read nutrition labels on packaged foods so that you can make healthier food choices. Pay attention to serving sizes. Many products list serving sizes that are less than what most people consume at a single sitting. You may be eating two or three times more calories than you think.

Eating five to nine servings of fresh fruits and vegetables each day is one important way to improve overall health.

www.usatoday.com

USA TODAY

Life
SECTION D

October 29, 2009

From the Pages of USA TODAY

Make the healthy diet choice the easy choice

Study finds that getting a weight-loss partner helps, too

Dieters can boost their weight loss if they clean up their act at home and get a partner to lose weight with them, a new study shows.

If you want to trim down, you should set up your home to make the healthy choice the easy choice, says Amy Gorin, assistant professor of psychology at the University of Connecticut.

She presented her research at the annual meeting of the Obesity Society, a group of weight-loss researchers and professionals.

Gorin and colleagues recruited 201 overweight and obese people and divided them into two groups.

Participants in one group got a six-month behavioral weight-loss program that emphasized a low-fat, low-calorie diet and moderate-intensity physical activity. They met weekly with weight-loss experts and learned how to keep food journals and work through tempting eating situations.

The other group got the same weekly weight-loss program with professional help. They also:

- Had an overweight partner participate in the weight-loss program with them. This was either a spouse or another adult who lived in the same home.
- Were given a piece of exercise equipment (a treadmill or exercise bike), bathroom scales, a full-length mirror, healthy cooking and fitness magazines and smaller dinner plates that were about the size of salad plates.
- Were encouraged to watch less television.

At the end of six months, dieters with a partner and extra equipment at home lost an average of 20 pounds [9 kg]; their partners also lost a substantial amount of weight. Dieters in the weight-loss advice group lost about 15 pounds [7 kg].

"Making concrete and real changes to the home make it much easier to stick with a healthful eating and exercise program," Gorin says.

—Nanci Hellmich

- Get moving! Physical activity can help you reach and keep a healthy weight. It also improves mood and thinking habits. Sixty to 90 minutes of daily moderate physical activity is recommended for most teenagers.
- Follow your progress weekly by tracking your food intake and physical activity. Keep tweaking the two until you begin to see progress toward your goals of healthy weight and increased vigor.
- If others in your family or among your friends are eating unhealthily and not exercising, try to get them on board too. Healthy behaviors are easier to keep up when those closest to you follow similar routines.

Exercise is an important part of becoming and staying healthy.

Adopting these recommendations may not bring quick results. But they lead to lifelong healthy habits. Long-term weight problems may also need professional advice and support before they can be brought under control. In such circumstances, talking honestly with your pediatrician or family doctor about how and where to start is an essential first step. It's never too late to start leading a healthy life by taking steps toward a healthy weight.

GLOSSARY

amino acids: the building blocks of proteins

anorexia nervosa: compulsive self-imposed starvation, related to underlying psychological reasons

appetite: a psychological desire for or interest in food or water

atherosclerosis: a disorder of the arteries in which the blood vessels become clogged with fatty deposits or plaque, causing higher-than-healthy blood pressure and ultimately increasing risk of stroke and heart attack. The condition is closely associated with increased weight and obesity.

binge eating: an eating disorder that involves periodic episodes of intensive eating (usually junk foods)

body mass index (BMI): a measure of body weight relative to height. BMI can be used to determine if a person is at a healthy weight, underweight, overweight, or obese.

bulimia: an eating disorder that involves alternating episodes of bingeing and purging (forced vomiting and/or use of laxatives)

calorie: a unit of heat or energy

carbohydrate: an important source of dietary energy. Some carbohydrates are "simple" and are found in sugars. "Complex" carbohydrates include both starches and fiber or cellulose.

cholesterol: a fatlike substance that is made in the body and is also found in many of the animal foods people eat, including meat, fish, poultry, foods fried in animal oils, eggs, and dairy products. Cholesterol is carried in the bloodstream and becomes a health problem when it accumulates in arteries to raise blood pressure and increase the risk of heart disease.

depression: a persistent mood of sadness, despair, and discouragement, which can be a symptom of many mental and physical disorders. Depression is often associated with obesity and eating disorders.

diabetes, type 1: a disease caused when the pancreas fails to produce insulin and therefore glucose is unable to enter cells. This results in increased levels of glucose circulating in the blood (hyperglycemia). Type 1 diabetes usually develops in childhood or adolescence, which is why it is sometimes also called juvenile diabetes. It is not caused by environmental factors, and people with type 1 must take insulin.

diabetes, type 2 (adult-onset diabetes): a disease caused by the body's inability to recognize its own insulin or to keep pace with its insulin needs, sometimes due to obesity

diet: what a person eats and drinks; also, any type of eating plan that has a desired goal such as weight loss

eating disorder: any chronic pattern of eating that inclines individuals to eat in ways that do not support their health. These include anorexia, bulimia, and binge eating.

empty calories: calories obtained from foods that have little or no nutritional value but are high in calories due to their sugars and fats. Many snack foods fit this description.

energy balance: when the amount of energy, measured in calories, that a person eats is about equal to the amount of energy, also measured in calories, that the person expends (the energy it takes to breathe, circulate blood, digest food, and be physically active). Whenever caloric intake is regularly greater than energy expenditure, a person gains weight. Reverse the equation and the individual loses weight.

fat: a major source of energy in the diet, with more than twice the number of calories per gram as proteins and carbohydrates. Fats are essential nutrients but must be eaten in moderation to avoid weight gain and health concerns.

hunger: a physical feeling of emptiness in the stomach due to a lack of food

insulin: a hormone in the body that helps move glucose (sugar) from the blood to muscles and other tissues where it is the main source of energy. People with diabetes either lack insulin altogether or are insulin-resistant. This means they produce insulin, but their body's cells are unable to use it.

leptin: a hormone that appears to have a central role in fat metabolism

liposuction: a cosmetic procedure for removing unwanted fat deposits under the skin through the use of surgically inserted suction tubes and high vacuum pressure

metabolism: the chemical process by which the body converts food into energy for such functions as digestion, respiration, and temperature regulation. Metabolic rate varies somewhat among individuals, depending on genetics and levels of activity, and contributes to differences in people's ability to gain and lose weight.

nutrients: any of the basic components of a diet, including carbohydrates, proteins, fats, vitamins, and minerals

nutrition: the process of nourishing or being nourished, especially as it relates to food; also the science associated with identifying and tracking what foods the body needs

obesity: a condition in which an individual has a high percentage of body fat. A person is considered obese if he or she has a BMI of 30 or higher. A BMI of 40 or more, or 100 pounds (45 kg) over average weight, is termed morbid obesity. This condition is considered medically disabling and likely to shorten life expectancy.

overweight: a body weight greater than is considered healthy for one's height; a BMI of 25 to 30

protein: one of the three nutrients that provide calories to the body and that are essential in building bone, muscle, skin, and blood. Proteins are found in foods such as meat, fish, poultry, eggs, dairy products, beans, and nuts.

satiety signal: an internal signal—a kind of hunger thermostat—that signals the brain when the stomach is full

serving size: a measured amount of any food upon which nutritional and calorie estimates are based

set point: the point at which body weight and metabolism stabilize, given a consistent pattern of eating, activity, and behavior. Diets can change metabolic rate and set point, but only after considerable resistance on the part of the body.

sleep apnea: a condition associated with being overweight, in which fat deposits in the tongue and neck interfere with breathing during sleep

RESOURCES

American Diabetes Association (ADA)
http://www.diabetes.org/

The ADA website provides information on diabetes and lifestyle issues associated with the disease. The Living with Diabetes section includes information for parents and kids on coping with everyday situations (such as school, parties, dating, and driving).

Let's Move
http://www.letsmove.gov

In February 2010, First Lady Michelle Obama launched this national initiative to reduce childhood obesity. The goals of the program are creating a healthy start for children; empowering parents and caregivers; providing healthy food in schools; improving access to healthy, affordable foods for all Americans; and increasing physical activity among children.

My Pyramid
http://www.mypyramid.gov/

This website is maintained by the U.S. Department of Agriculture. It explains the *Dietary Guidelines for Americans–2010,* based on the four basic food groups, and describes what goes into a healthy diet. The site also includes interactive tools to assess your fitness and eating habits and help you build a personalized plan for eating and living better.

Overeaters Anonymous (OA)
http://www.oa.org/

This free program helps people to overcome compulsive eating habits. Through group meetings with other compulsive eaters, the OA approach addresses physical, emotional, and spiritual well-being. OA does not promote a specific diet. The website provides information on finding meetings in your area. The Youth in OA page has a quiz to help you determine if you are a compulsive eater.

TeensHealth: Food and Fitness
http://www.kidshealth.org/teen/food_fitness/

Sponsored by the Nemours Foundation, this website includes a Food & Fitness section with information on teen weight management and healthy nutrition. Click on "Expert Answers" for answers to frequently asked question about teen health, including dieting and weight.

SELECTED BIBLIOGRAPHY

Berg, Frances M. *Underage and Overweight: America's Childhood Obesity Crisis*. New York: Hatherleigh Press, 2004.

Dalton, Sharron. *Our Overweight Children: What Parents, Schools, and Communities Can Do to Control the Fatness Epidemic*. Berkeley: University of California Press, 2004.

Favor, Lesli J. *Weighing In*. New York: Marshall Cavendish, 2010.

Gratzer, Walter. *Terrors of the Table: The Curious History of Nutrition*. New York: Oxford University Press, 2005.

Litin, Scott C., ed. "Nutrition and Healthy Eating." In *Mayo Clinic Family Health Book*, 4th ed. Rochester, MN: Mayo Clinic, 2010.

Rimm, Sylvia. *Rescuing the Emotional Lives of Overweight Children: What Our Kids Go Through—And How We Can Help*. Emmaus, PA: Rodale Press, 2004.

Tartamella, Lisa, Elaine Herscher, and Chris Woolston. *Generation Extra Large: Rescuing Our Children from the Epidemic of Obesity*. New York: Basic Books, 2004.

FURTHER READING AND WEBSITES

Books

Bellenir, Karen. *Diet Information for Teens: Health Tips about Diet and Nutrition*. Detroit: Omnigraphics, 2006.

Brynie, Faith Hickman. *101 Questions about Food and Digestion*. Minneapolis: Twenty-First Century Books, 2002.

Johnson, Rebecca L., *Genetics*. Minneapolis: Twenty-First Century Books, 2006.

Ojeda, Linda. *Safe Dieting for Teens*. 2nd ed. Alameda, CA: Hunter House, 2008.

Silverstein, Alvin, Virginia Silverstein, and Laura Silverstein Nunn. *DNA*. Minneapolis: Twenty-First Century Books, 2009.

———. *Heart Disease*. Minneapolis: Twenty-First Century Books, 2006.

Expand learning beyond the printed book. Download free, complementary educational resources for this book from our website, www.lerneresource.com

Websites

Centers for Disease Control and Prevention (CDC)
Division of Nutrition, Physical Activity and Obesity
http://www.cdc.gov/nccdphp/dnpao/index.html

The mission of this division of the CDC is "to lead strategic public health efforts to prevent and control obesity, chronic disease, and other health conditions through regular physical activity and good nutrition." The site includes information on healthy weight, nutrition, physical activity, and statistics about overweight individuals and obesity in the United States.

Mayo Clinic
www.mayoclinic.com

The Mayo Clinic's mission is to "inspire hope and contribute to the health and well-being" of their patients. The clinic's website has a Healthy Lifestyle section with information on nutrition, fitness, and weight loss (http://www.mayoclinic.com/health/HealthyLivingIndex/HealthyLivingIndex).

Obesity in America
http://www.obesityinamerica.org/

Sponsored by the Endocrine Society, an international organization for endocrinologists (doctors who specialize in the endocrine system, which produces hormones), this website has information for the general public and the media regarding scientific trends and advancements that they hope will lead to a "slimmer, fitter America."

The Surgeon General's Vision for a Healthy and Fit Nation 2010
http://www.surgeongeneral.gov/library/obesityvision/obesityvision2010.pdf

U.S. surgeon general Regina M. Benjamin's statement of the U.S. Department of Health and Human Services' goals for stopping the obesity epidemic in the United States is available at this site.

Weight-Control Information Network (WIN)
http://www.win.niddk.nih.gov

WIN is a service of the National Institutes of Health (National Institute of Diabetes and Digestive and Kidney Diseases). Their website provides information on weight control, obesity, physical activity, and related nutritional issues for the general public, health professionals, and the media.

INDEX

ABOUT THE AUTHOR

Wendy Murphy is editorial director of Onward Publishing, a health communications company, as well as a freelance author of more than two dozen books in the medical and behavioral fields. She has written about topics ranging from nuclear medicine and the workings of the human brain to modern drug development and the history of physical therapy. Recent books include *Orphan Diseases, New Hope for Rare Medical Conditions; Asthma;* and *Spare Parts, from Peg Legs to Gene Splices*, a history of medical repair devices. She lives in Connecticut.

PHOTO ACKNOWLEDGMENTS

The images in this book are used with the permission of: © SPL/Photo Researchers, Inc., pp. 1, 3, 27; © Lawrence Weslowski Jr/Dreamstime.com, p. 5; © Steven Peters/ Riser/Getty Images, p. 9; © Edyta Pawlowska/Dreamstime.com, p. 11; © Sergio Vila/Dreamstime.com, p. 14; © Jack Gruber/USA TODAY, p. 15; AP Photo/Mark Humphrey, p. 19; © Foodie Photography/FoodPix/Getty Images, p. 23; © Hybrid Medical Animation/Photo Researchers, Inc., p. 25; © Paul Harris/Stone/Getty Images, p. 28; © Fotoluminate/Dreamstime.com, p. 31; © Monkey Business Images/ Dreamstime.com, p. 33; The Art Archive/National Anthropological Museum Mexico/ Gianni Dagli Orti, p. 35; © SSPL/The Image Works, p. 38; © Hulton Archive/Getty Images, p. 39; © Ken James/Bloomberg via Getty Images, p. 40; © Muhs/Caro/ Alamy, p. 44; AP Photo/M. Spencer Green, p. 47; © Tim Dillon/USA TODAY, p. 51; © Norman Y. Lono/USA TODAY, p. 52; © Jovani Carlo Gorospe/Dreamstime.com, p. 53; © Danicek/Dreamstime.com, p. 55; © Dennis MacDonald/Alamy, p. 57; American Idol Prod./19 Television/Fox TV Network/Fremantle Media North America/ The Kobal Collection/Micellotta, Frank, p. 58; AP Photo/PRNewsFoto/The Milk Processor Education Program, p. 59; © Frederick C. Skvara, MD/Visuals Unlimited, Inc., p. 66 (left); © Biodisc/Visuals Unlimited, Inc., p. 66 (right); © Eileen Blass/ USA TODAY, p. 67; © Karen A. Tam/USA TODAY, p. 73; © Ralph Hutchings/Visuals Unlimited, Inc., p. 75; © Howard Sandler/Dreamstime.com, p. 78; AP Photo/Wilfredo Lee, p. 84; © Mary Evans Picture Library/The Image Works, p. 86; © Martin Lee/ mediablitzimages (uk) Limited/Alamy, p. 88; © Justin Sullivan/Getty Images, p. 90; © Network Photographers/Alamy, p. 91; © Michelle Del Guercio/Photo Researchers, Inc., p. 95; © Loisjoy Thurstun/Bubbles Photography/Alamy, p. 97; © Acik/ Dreamstime.com, p. 99; © Stephan Gladieu/Getty Images, p. 101.

Front cover: © SPL/Photo Researchers, Inc.

Main body text set in USA TODAY Roman 10/15.